Reflections on

When in doubt, get back to basics. That's a solid approach to any pursuit, but especially in our spiritual walk with the Lord. In *The Simplest Thing...*, Cassie has penned an encouraging reminder that when life seems overwhelming, the simplest and best thing you can do is concentrate on the basics of your relationship with Him—and everything else will fall into proper perspective.

Jim Daly
President | Focus on the Family

In the midst of the complications of life—relational challenges, financial struggles, health issues, relentlessly terrible news, etc.—it's easy to lose sight of the most important thing: simply abiding in the Lord and allowing Him to abide in me. I need a reminder from time to time (we *all* do, to be honest), and this book is one of those necessary reminders. I so appreciate Cassie's honesty, transparency, and vulnerability in each page of *The Simplest Thing...* It has challenged me to get back to the roots of my relationship with the Lord. To slow down and enjoy Him and invite Him into the messiness of life—the joys and the sorrows, the mundane and the exhilarating—*all* of it. It serves as a sort of necessary spiritual recalibration. This isn't a book designed to be rushed through in a single sitting ... to get the most out of it, I encourage you to slowly savor and reflected upon it, page by page and chapter by chapter. And as you ask the Holy Spirit to speak to you, I know you will be incredibly transformed and blessed!

S. George Thomas
Executive Pastor | Gateway Church

In a world where there is so much noise, Cassie invites us in to learn how following the Lord is simple—not necessarily easy, but simple. *The Simplest Thing…* shares her words, stories, and Scripture to encourage you in your journey to invite Jesus into your joys, sorrows, and grief. I highly recommend this beautiful work!

Holly Newton
Author and Founder | Exhale Women

Weaving through the entirety of *The Simplest Thing…* are the incredible stories of life after loss, restoration, redemption, forgiveness, and hope. Cassie has an incredible way of intertwining honest feelings with biblical truth and practical application. Each chapter ends with a question, prayer, and reflection which encourages the reader to pause and reflect on how they can return to the solid foundation of a relationship with the Lord—no matter what is going on in the world around them and in their personal lives. This inspiring and motivating book is one that you will want to pick up and read over and over!

Karen Harmon
Bettertogether.tv
Speaker, Writer, Business Owner

From the beginning pages of *The Simplest Thing…*, Cassie's personal story spoke to me. When she explains the idea of her time spent with the Lord not always feeling personal, a light bulb went off. I could never put into words the struggle I've felt at times when reading my Bible or a devotional book. I devoted my time, and my heart was in the right place, but my feelings of overwhelm prevented the real work from being done. The idea of simplicity and getting to square one with Jesus is a concept that every Christian can benefit from—a concept that is not touched on enough in our fast-paced, ever-changing world! Cassie details cultivating a relationship with Jesus in a way that maybe we haven't taken the time to fully execute. In missing those steps, we are missing out on truly understanding the Lord's promises and experiencing life through Him—*with Him*—as He intended. Cassie's words have me taking a step back in my life only to take steps forward in my walk with Jesus.

Dina Deleasa-Gonsar
Creator, Writer, and Television Personality | Dish It Girl
Television Personality | Married to Jonas

The Simplest Thing...

The Simplest Thing...

Returning to the Foundation of Your Relationship with the Lord

Cassie Cooper

The Simplest Thing...

ISBN 978-0-578-98261-8 (paperback edition)

Unless otherwise indicated, all Scripture is taken from the New Living Translation (NLT) © 1996 by Tyndale House Publishers, Inc.

Scripture quotations marked NIV are taken from the New International Version (NIV) © 1984 by Biblica, Inc.

Scripture quotations marked NKJV are taken from the New King James Version (NKJV) © 1982 by Thomas Nelson, Inc.

Edited by Katie Smith.
Cover design and interior formatting by Christy Kaneta.
Photography by Jackie Cooper.

To my sister, Tessa. I don't think I'll ever understand why you went so soon, but I do know that in losing you, the Lord taught me The Simplest Thing....

To my family. You lived this journey with me. Thank you for encouraging me, cheering me on, reading and re-reading my work, and praying me through the most difficult seasons. I couldn't have done this without you.

CONTENTS

Before We Begin...

My friends, thank you so much for choosing to join me on my journey of discovering the simplest thing. There are two ways you can read this book:

1. If you're feeling down or need some encouragement, pick it up and read a chapter, two, or three. This is the kind of book that can be read whenever you need it.

OR

2. You can take your time working through the thoughts in the following pages. I've added a few steps you can take at the end of each chapter to fully dive into what the Lord has taught me over the past few years. There's a space for reflection and journaling if you choose, a prayer to pray over yourself, and a reminder from the chapter to simply ponder. You're welcome to even cut it out of the book and put it up somewhere as a clearly visible reminder.

This Is Simply Me...

I would say I'm a pretty simple girl, and I think those who know me would say the same. It doesn't take much to make me happy: a good cup of coffee in the sunshine, getting lost in an inviting book, authentic street tacos, really bad dad jokes, a cable-knit blanket, sitting by an open window when it's pouring out so I can smell the rain, meaningful conversations, or anything lavender could just about do the job of adding satisfaction to any day. Simplicity. I like it, and I tend to live my life that way.

Merriam-Webster defines simplicity as the state of being simple, uncomplicated, or uncompounded. That sounds so appealing to me.

Naturally, you could also say I'm a black-and-white thinker. I like things clear-cut, I love a good plan, and I prefer to know my role in it. I like knowing what I'm supposed to do so I can put it on my list and check it off when I'm done.

But over the years, I've found that the most significant piece of my life is often far from a clear-cut, well-defined plan with A-B-C action steps. You see, the most significant and important part of my life is my relationship with Jesus. And if you know much about following Jesus, you certainly know we are called to lean not on our own understanding, but instead trust in Him and He will direct our paths (Proverbs 3:5–6).

When we follow Jesus, we can rest assured that He always has a plan (Jeremiah 29:11), but more often than not, He chooses not to let us in on the checklist to accomplish the plan. This truth has been a harder one for me to swallow, if I can be perfectly honest. I like to know the plan, I love getting progress updates along the way, and I want to check things off of the list. (Truth be told, sometimes I put something I've already done on the list just so I can cross it off and feel even more accomplished.)

Learning slowly but surely that I will rarely know the plan and am thus required to trust and take the next step has undoubtedly been a growing experience. But what would faith be if we knew the whole plan? I know this in my head, but letting this truth settle in my heart has been a much longer process. I once heard that the longest distance your faith has to travel is the 12 inches from your head to your heart—how true.

In my mind, if I don't know the plan, then ...

How could I go about accomplishing it?
What steps do I need to take?
What's next?
How should I prepare?
Am I wasting time?

Suddenly, the questions take over, and everything seems out of my control and oh, so complicated! But looking back on these moments revealed that I mistook my perceived lack of a plan and my definite lack of control for the lack of simplicity. I'm learning we can easily get caught up in all of the details and miss the heart—the simple truth—behind our relationship with the Lord.

Right now, I'm learning that following the Lord is actually quite simple—not easy—*simple*. I'm learning that genuine relationship with the Lord, in fact, hinges on something unbelievably simple: inviting Him in. Inviting Him into the joy of celebration. Inviting Him into the sorrow and grief of loss. Inviting Him into the bitterness of disappointment. Inviting Him into the simultaneous beauty and messiness of life to be my Source, my Strength, my All. I feel like a child learning all of this again, but let me tell you, it's been one of the sweetest and most satisfying lessons. Stick with me, and if you let me, I want to share what I'm discovering on this journey of learning the simplest thing ....

And here we go ...

chapter 1

Simply Discovering Simplicity...

This season has been one of learning how to return to square one in my relationship with the Lord. As I write this, it's been more than three years since I graduated from college. While I was thrilled to cross that milestone, no one really prepares you for the mountain of transition afterward. It's a season filled with excitement, hopes and dreams, and independence. It's also full of uncertainty, loneliness, and spending a lot of money on things like dish soap and shower curtains. You're trying to navigate adulthood, succeed in your job, pay your bills, and balance your relationship with the Lord while still spending time with people, so you don't become a hermit.

A few months into post-grad, I felt like I was starting to get into a routine. I had moved back to Tulsa, Oklahoma, the hometown of my alma mater; I was living with some close friends; and to my pleasant surprise, I found myself successfully keeping my head above water. There were still stressful days, but overall, life was fairly decent. There was a rhythm. And oh, I love rhythms. Then in one day, my decent routine shifted.

On Thursday, September 6, 2018, my life was forever altered. On my way into work, I got a phone call from my parents, who lived in Colorado, relaying the news that my older sister had an allergic reaction to medication and was in the ICU. She was on life support, and it was a waiting game. I could do nothing but go to work and pray for my sister as I went about my day. My parents prepared to fly to Arizona where my sister was in the hospital, and we all awaited test results. It was a painfully slow day with a roller-coaster of emotions.

Later that afternoon, I got a call from my dad with what I assumed would be an update on my sister or their travel plans. Instead, my dad shared the news that my cousin, who was like an older brother to me growing up, had been killed that morning in a car accident. I've never fainted in my life, but I think that was the closest I've come. Our entire family was shaken; none of us had ever lost a family member that suddenly. And in one day, we were left reeling with the news of one sudden loss and waiting for information on another whose condition was looking increasingly more devastating as time went on.

I spent the next several days grieving the loss of my cousin, trying to coordinate flights to his funeral, and waiting for news about my sister. The reports trickled in ….

She has lost all brain activity on her left and right sides ….

If she does wake up, she will be a vegetable ….

She stated in her will that she would never want to be kept alive by life support ….

On Monday, four days later, I prepared to fly out for my cousin's funeral, which would be held the following day. Monday was also the day it was decided my sister would be removed from life support. There was so much prayer before anyone could come to peace with that decision. Even now, looking back, by the goodness of the Lord, it's already plain to see that my sister's life has become a beautiful pillar of restoration and God's grace.

The doctors scheduled her unhooking during the middle

of my flight. I said my goodbyes to her before I boarded the plane, and by the time I landed, she had passed. She went quickly and peacefully, and that in itself was a blessing. With her lack of brain activity, it could have been lengthy and painful.

The next morning, one of my brothers, my other sister, and I attended our cousin's funeral. That was by far one of the hardest days I've ever had to live through. We were separated from half of our family, grieving the fresh loss of our sister, grieving the loss of our cousin, and all while sitting in the same funeral home where our sister's service would be held a week and a half later. That day and the day of my sister's funeral are days that I never, ever wish to relive.

Overwhelmed by Grief

The cloud of grief surrounding those days and the days to follow made everything seem complicated and increasingly challenging, lacking the simplicity I so deeply craved. And right in the midst of that cloud of grief, I moved for the second time in three months, changed roommates, switched positions at my job twice, and said goodbye as dear friends moved away.

It seemed as though I blinked, and everything changed. My life had gone from a fairly decent routine surrounded by loving and caring people to a haphazard whirlwind characterized by loss, grief, loneliness, and the unknown. There were so many things I wanted—needed—to process with the Lord, but I could never figure out where to begin, so I simply didn't start. I still spent time with the Lord, but truthfully, it wasn't personal. I read my Bible and maybe a section from a devotional book, but I was so overwhelmed I couldn't seem to find the words to process what was going through my heart and mind.

He Answered with Simplicity

After a couple of months of this, I finally told God my struggle. I honestly expressed to Him that I wanted to share—in fact, I craved that intimacy with Him—but I was too overwhelmed even to know where to begin. And at that moment, I felt the Lord speak so clearly to my heart. He didn't give me all the answers I was hoping for, and He didn't let me in on the plan—or even the next step, for that matter. He simply said, "Invite Me in."

In an instant, I caught a glimpse of that simplicity I missed so dearly. It was as if the Father said to not even pray about all of the other things right then but to just take it back to square one and invite Him into the moment—what a beautiful picture of relationship. Before the Lord can revolutionize our worlds, change our hearts, or even give us the next step, we have to have relationship with Him. And the most incredible part? He took the first step. He loved us first (1 John 4:19). Now, we get to choose to love Him in return.

He Loved Us First

The Christmas after my sister passed, I attended an Advent service at my church where the pastor explained so well this amazing love that the Lord has for us. This love is what drove the Lord to sacrifice absolutely everything just so He could have a relationship with us.

The pastor described it through a story: *once there was a king. This king was the most powerful king to ever rule on the earth; he was prosperous, victorious, respected, and loved.*

When it came time for the king to marry, he fell deeply in love with a poor woman who lived and worked in the village near his kingdom. His advisors counseled the king to bring the woman in and command her to marry him. The king was unsettled by this idea, for he loved the woman so deeply. He wanted nothing more than her genuine love in return. He knew that if he took the woman away from her life and her home and commanded her to marry him, she would obey, for no one had ever dared to disobey the king. He knew she would respect him and do as he said, but he knew she would live the life of a servant merely doing her duty to the king.

Because the king sincerely desired her love in return, he chose to renounce his throne, give up his power and wealth, and become a common man. He moved to the village and wooed the woman with whom he was in love, and she did indeed give her love in return. The king had given up all he had and all he was to win the woman's genuine affection, and to the king, it was all worth it.

This is the simple yet profound relationship that the Lord so deeply desires to have with us. He never wanted us to love Him from a place of debt or servanthood; rather, He wants our genuine affection and love. And this is all He wants. No bait-and-switch, no fine print, simply our devotion. He wants us to make the conscious decision to return His love and invest in relationship with Him. Step one? Inviting Him in.

Abiding in Our Source

John 15:5 says He is the vine, and we are the branches. If we abide in Him and He in us, then we will bear much fruit, for apart from Him, we can do nothing. This is the foundation of our relationship with the Lord ... inviting Him in and abiding in Him. The branch doesn't try to bear fruit by its own effort. And it definitely cannot stretch its arms out in growth toward the sun without the nourishment and strength from the vine. If the branch is cut off from the vine at any point, it will immediately cease to live, much less provide fruit.

The branch is entirely dependent upon the vine for every good thing. But the thing I find most beautiful about this relationship is the branch doesn't have to *try* to remain dependent upon the vine; it just *is*. The branch isn't trying to cling to the vine, it's not working hard to be nourished by the vine, and it's not painstakingly rearranging itself for a better grip.

I can try with all of my might to dig myself out from underneath this mountain of grief. I can strive to find healing and emotional health. I can cling to practices and exercises that will help my heart move toward restoration. But if I do any of these things *before* abiding or *instead of* abiding, my efforts will be ultimately fruitless. As I choose to abide in the Father, His work begins to move in and through me, teaching me lessons and taking me leaps and bounds further than I could ever go in my own strength. The branch simply abides in the vine, receives the nourishment from the vine, and from that, it accomplishes its good purpose: bearing fruit.

He Is Our Sustenance

Jesus gives another picture of this dependence upon Him for life in John 6:47–58. He says that He is the bread of life, and anyone who eats of this bread will never die. He even goes on to say that unless we "'eat the flesh of the Son of Man and drink His blood, [we] cannot have eternal life within [us]. But anyone who eats [His] flesh and drinks [His] blood has eternal life, and [He] will raise that person at the last day'" (John 6:53–54). At first glance, that seems a little extreme—graphic, even. But Jesus isn't talking about literally eating His flesh and drinking His blood—for us, that's impossible. Instead, He made the poignant case that *He* is our life sustenance. As naturally as we eat and drink to sustain our physical life, we must receive nourishment from Jesus to sustain our spiritual life.

Relationship Really Is That Simple

This is the picture of relationship with Jesus: inviting Him in, resting in Him, and receiving our nourishment from

Him. While this act is often far from easy, I'm learning that it's incredibly simple. The work to which we are called is to believe in Him (John 6:29) and abide in Him (John 15:5), and He will work in and through us. When we extend that simple invitation, we are inviting Him to do what He does best. As we abide, we, like the branch, simply become the conduit of His work.

Yet how many times do we overcomplicate this relationship? We think to ourselves, "Surely it cannot be *that* simple—inviting Him in and abiding in Him. I have to study, I have to learn, I have to practice, I have to pray about *all of these things* …." There are a great many things we have yet to learn about the Lord. Truths we long to uncover. Promises we have not yet claimed. Prayers we must learn to pray. But none of these things—not one—can come before inviting Him in and abiding in Him, for out of this secret place of abiding flows all of the Christian life and life to the fullest. Apart from Him, we can do nothing. Everything our Lord asks of us He also supplies to us in relationship with Him. He says not to grieve as those who have no hope, and He is the One who comforts our hearts. He says fear not, and He is the One who supplies the peace. He says be strong and courageous, and He is the One who strengthens our spirits. He says to forgive, and He is the One who supplies the grace to do it. He says love your enemies, and He is the One who fills us with His own love to accomplish the task.

Many things require discipline, study, and practice in the Christian life. For although our spirits are transformed at the moment of salvation, our minds and our bodies are the same. We have the same habits, the same tendencies, and the same wounds that need healing. And the start of all of this is the invitation we extend to our Father: "Come, abide with me. I invite You into this moment, this moment right here and now." As we continue to extend this invitation, we watch the transformation unfold from our spirits to our minds and our bodies.

Our First Calling

The Lord has called us to a great many things in this life. He has called us to trust, surrender, be still, praise, hope ... but deep in each of these callings is first the entreating to invite Him in. His desire is for us to invite Him into these moments with the trust that He can work it out in our lives. He longs for us to be still in His presence so that He can transform our hearts. He wants to be the first object of our hope so that He can bring His best in His time. Every single step of the Christian life must find its footing in that simple invitation.

Looking back, I see that one of the many things this season is teaching me is that I recognize my desperate need for the Lord in a way that I haven't before. I can clearly and distinctly see that I must abide in Him and have relationship with Him to survive. And this all starts with an invitation. There is no 10-year plan to a better relationship with God, no list of outlined action steps to get me there, and no creative brainstorming sessions to try and figure it all out. There is one step. And that one step is what must be repeated over and over again as I learn to abide in Him, draw my strength and nourishment from Him, and then bear fruit because I am connected to the vine. When the rest of my life seems so overwhelming and complicated, I am continually in awe that the most incredible relationship I will ever invest in promises a start that is just so simple and infallible: inviting Him in.

What things do I need to set aside today so that I can simply invite the Lord in?

_____

_____

_____

_____

Father, would You help me by the power of Your Holy Spirit to surrender every weight and care to You? Today, I choose to invite You in and simply abide in You. Amen.

Before the Lord can
revolutionize our worlds,
change our hearts,
or even give us
the next step,
we have to have
relationship with Him.

chapter 2
Simply Building Relationship...

"Lord, I invite You in." This simple invitation we extend to the Lord is a deliberate act of our will. The decision will always be up to us to invite Him into our moments, our days, our lives. One of the things I find most beautiful about the Lord is that He created us with a will, knowing we would misuse it. He knew full well that we would choose to make selfish decisions, permeate our lives with pride, and reject Him daily; yet, He was so deeply enthralled with letting us also *choose* to love Him. I never cease to be overwhelmed by that amount of love.

I think if we were to be honest with ourselves, we truly believe the Lord loves us and wants to be included in our lives. But subconsciously, we also think He doesn't really care about being brought into the minuscule and mundane: a project at work, making dinner, or doing laundry. We want to bring the Lord into the joys, thanking Him for His blessings! We also want to bring Him into the deep sorrows, asking for His peace and comfort when we can't see the sun through the clouds. But we so often forget He wants to be part of *every* piece of our lives. He wants to be invited into all of it.

He's Always There ...
Now before I go on, let me be perfectly clear, I fully

believe the Lord is always by our side, and He never leaves us. It's scriptural.

> Joshua 1:9 says, "'Have I not commanded you? Be strong and courageous. Do not be afraid; do not be discouraged, for the LORD your God will be *with you* wherever you go'" (NIV).

> Deuteronomy 31:8 says, "'The Lord himself goes before you and will be *with you*; He will never leave you nor forsake you. Do not be afraid; do not be discouraged'" (NIV).

> And the end of Matthew 28:20 says, "'And surely I am *with you* always, to the very end of the age'" (NIV).

These are just three examples of the more than 35 found in Scripture (depending on the version and specific phrase you search). We can believe what His Word says. He has promised us that He will always be right by our sides (Matthew 28:20), He can't break His promises (Hebrews 6:18), and His Word is truth (John 17:17). But I also believe that someone can be with you all of the time and still not be part of what you are doing.

... but He's Longing for an Invitation

You can spend hours upon hours with a friend, but you may not always be involved in what they are thinking or doing. As I sit in my room and write this, my roommates are home. If someone were to ask if I were with them, I would truthfully answer yes! But we're not interacting at the moment, I'm not participating in what they are doing, and they are not part of the project I'm currently working on. Why? Because I haven't invited them in. I believe it is much the same with the Lord. Revelation 3:20 says that the Lord stands at the door and knocks. He's there, but He doesn't barge on in uninvited. He is a gentleman who waits for us to open the door and invite Him to come in. The rest of the verse promises that if we open the door and invite Him in, He will come in, and as the New Living Translation puts it, *"share a meal together as friends."* What a beautiful picture of relationship.

The Lord has given it all up to engage in relationship with us ... to allow us to choose to love Him in return. Even though He has given everything for us, He still asks us to open the door and extend an invitation for Him to be part of our lives. And I'm not just talking about the moment of salvation! I believe that initial invitation is the most significant and meaningful one we will ever extend to the Lord, but please listen carefully: *that is not the only time we invite Him in.*

Every Moment of Every Day

I believe at the moment of salvation we are sealed, and our names are written in the Lamb's Book of Life (Revelation 3:5). From that point on, the Lord will never leave or forsake us. But walking out our salvation as Christ-followers means a daily, moment-by-moment process of inviting Him into the journey. He is always with me, but I want so much more than that. I want Him to be part of everything that I am doing, and I want to be *part* of everything He is doing. All of that starts with just opening the door and inviting Him in.

Sometimes all I can say is, "Lord, I invite You into this moment," and I know He is there (even if I can't always *feel* it). Sometimes it's more specific: inviting Him into my seemingly unsolvable problem, inviting Him into my frustration, or inviting Him into my moment of sipping coffee in the sunshine. But I believe it all starts with saying, "Lord, I invite You into this moment today."

Investing in Relationship

Now, I've been talking a lot about inviting the Lord into our daily lives—inviting Him into the small moments, the times we're spending with Him, or the joys and sorrows. I believe inviting the Lord into any situation is the key foundation of our relationships with Him, but we cultivate that relationship by investing our time into it.

I was recently reminded that relationship with the Lord is a process that comes about through delighting in Him, dwelling in His presence, and abiding in Him. These are not fast-paced words; instead, they force us to slow our rapid pace and spend time in the presence of the Father. Just as the branch does not instantly bear fruit from being connected to the vine, so we also must invest time into abiding with our Source—our heavenly Father.

The more I think about it, I believe the Lord is a quality-time person. I'm sure you've heard of the different love languages: words of affirmation, physical touch, acts of service, gifts, and quality time. I think we could honor the Lord with almost all of these expressions of love toward Him (except perhaps physical touch ... I can't exactly give Him a hug right now), and the Lord would be pleased.

Interestingly enough, however, I could find examples in Scripture that place one of these demonstrations of love above the rest. The Lord does not need our words, for the heavens declare His glory, and the skies proclaim the work of His hands (Psalm 19:1). We cannot earn our salvation or honor Him merely by works, for then we would boast in ourselves and not in Him (Ephesians 2:9). The Lord does not require our gifts and sacrifices (Psalm 51:16), for He gave the ultimate Gift and Sacrifice.

But time after time in Scripture, I find commands of the Lord saying to "be still and know that [He is] God" (Psalm 46:10), entreating requests to come away to the secret place with Him (Psalm 91:1), and invitations to draw near to Him (James 4:8). This tells me something very significant about the heart of the Father: He does not desire relationship for what we can do for Him or for what we bring to the table; rather, He longs for relationship with us for *relationship's sake.*

Now please don't misunderstand; I believe the Lord is pleased when we serve Him, when we praise Him with our words, and when we honor Him with our gifts. But these declarations of love are not vital pieces of building relationship with us. He wants to invest quality time in relationships with us to meet with us, commune with us, and share life with us.

So How Should We Invest?

But what does this relationship time look like after we have initially invited Him into the moment? I think so often, we get stuck on a formal idea of "quiet time." Hear me out—I believe a scheduled and structured quiet time is important! I think there is something beautiful and healthy about setting aside time each day to invest in relationship with the Lord. Sometimes it requires sacrifice and discipline as committed relationships do, but this is neither the only time nor the only way we can (or should) invest in relationship with the Lord.

Think about it in terms of friendship. Picture your best friend. You may really enjoy spending time in the company of that friend. Still, I think we must honestly admit that if all you ever did with your friend was to invite them to sit at the same coffee shop, at the same table, and talk about the same things each day, it would get a little boring, and the relationship would likely not go much deeper. It is healthy for the relationship to have some kind of regularity, but it becomes stagnant when regularity is all there is to it.

Spending time with the Lord doesn't always have to look the same. We are not limited to reading a section of

Scripture, journaling about it, and closing with prayer. I know that for a time, I fell into the trap of thinking that was the only way to spend "real" time with the Lord. I felt guilty when I missed my reading in the morning and believed I couldn't *honestly* say I had spent time with the Lord that day. But let me tell you, that is a lie from the enemy to get you walking in shame and guilt. The Lord has created each of us uniquely and wired us to communicate in different ways. Just as we communicate differently with those around us, the Lord communicates differently and uniquely with each of us.

Robert Mulholland wrote an excellent book, *Invitation to a Journey*, on the very topic of spending vibrant time with the Lord. I recommend giving it a read if you want to dive deeper into the subject. In his book, he writes about how people are uniquely wired to spend time with the Lord in different yet life-giving ways. Some people may best connect with the Lord in nature, others through reading books of theology, and still others through creativity. No one way of connecting with the Lord is better than another; he merely points out that the Lord desires to relate with each person in their own unique way. I think that is one of the most beautiful pictures of the heart of the Father—He desires to meet us where we're at and connect with us in a way that we best connect. He desires *friendship* with us.

Friendship?

Travel with me for a moment on a train of thought that I recently had about friendship with the Lord. The week before Easter, I was sitting in a church service. It was Holy Week, a time when we remember the price our Savior paid—the immeasurable pain, the suffering, the grief—to restore our relationship to the Father. The time of remembrance starts solemn but ends with great joy.

I love Easter and everything surrounding it. I love the intentional space to recognize the work Christ did on the cross. I love that it happens (for those of us in the Northern Hemisphere, at least) in the spring—a time when death is giving way to new life. And I love celebrating the entire foundation of my faith—that Christ paid the ultimate price by dying a gruesome death and three days later rising from the dead so I could forever have a relationship with the Father through Him. This week is the entire foundation of all we believe.

In the service, the pastor preached a message about the Last Supper—the Passover meal Christ shared with His disciples on the night He would be betrayed. He shared all of the preparation leading up to that night; he also pointed out that Jesus and His disciples shared the Passover meal one night earlier than was traditionally celebrated. Jesus knew if He waited another night, He would not be able to share this last meal with His closest followers.

One piece of this message stood out to me, however, in a way it had not before. I love it when that happens—a passage I've heard hundreds of times since I was born, and I'm still learning new things about it. In Matthew 26:29, Jesus says He will not drink from the fruit of this vine (the wine) until the day that He drinks it new with His disciples in His Father's kingdom. Jesus knew this was the last meal He would share with His closest friends on this earth. If I knew that I was sharing my last meal with my closest friends, I think it would be a truly special time. A time to reminisce, a time to interact with one another, and a time to enjoy each other's presence. The Bible doesn't relay all of the conversations which took place that night, but I'd like to think that along with the meaningful and somber words of Jesus, there was also laughter and the sharing of stories.

The second part of that verse also stood out to me—this would be the last meal *until* the day Jesus and His disciples drink it new in the Father's kingdom. I thought to myself, what a fantastic reunion that must have been! When John finally entered the kingdom, and they were all together again, I can imagine them sitting down to a meal, sharing with one another, laughing, reminiscing—what a joyful and memorable time that must have been. I know Jesus certainly thinks differently than I do, and perspectives are different in Heaven, but I also know I would be overwhelmed with joy to be reunited with my closest friends.

As I was thinking about this in service, I thought to myself that Jesus must have felt an immense amount of joy to be reunited with His disciples—His closest friends on earth. As soon as the thought entered my mind, the Lord brought John 15:15 to mind:

> "'No longer do I call you servants ... I have called you *friends*'" (NKJV).

I felt the Lord whisper to my heart that He will be just as overjoyed when I arrive in Heaven, and He gets to sit down to a meal with me—His friend.

I believe we all view God and our relationships with Him in different lights. In *The Knowledge of the Holy*, A. W. Tozer writes, "What comes into our minds when we think about God is the most important thing about us." How we think about God defines how we live out our relationship with God after initially inviting Him in. I've always thought more of Him as a faithful God and loving Father. While that view defines how I see my relationship with Him, I can never forget there are so many other sides to the Lord. I think we often miss out on the fullness of relationship with God because we limit that relationship to our primary view of Him when He is so much more.

"Friend" has not always been my natural, default view

of God. But I think, lately, the Lord is telling me He wants me to see more of the side of God that says we are friends. I am *friends* with God. A friend is someone you share with, someone you trust, someone you laugh and cry with, someone you process with, and someone who brings you joy and comfort. The Hebrew word for "friend" is *philous*, which is translated as beloved, someone who is dear to you—a friend. Having a true friend—someone beloved and dear to you—is a rare gift and brings such pure joy. I have that in Christ.

The Feeling Is Mutual

Not only can I proceed with confidence knowing I can believe Christ is my friend, but I can also know with deep conviction that Christ sees me the same way. It's not one of those one-sided relationships where only one person sees the other as a friend—His friendship is mutual. In John 15:15, Jesus uses two different Greek verbs for the word "call." The first time He says He no longer calls us servants, He uses the word *lego* which means simply to speak or say. When He calls us *friends*, however, He uses the Greek verb *ereo*. *Ereo* means to say, declare, and promise. He declares us His friends, and His friendship is a promise.

Often it is easy to forget the multiple facets of God. When we examine the relationship we have with the Father, it's incredibly easy to get caught up in our primary view of Him—which is important!—but we lose sight of all that God is and all our relationship with Him can be. This is a lesson the Lord has me learning right now. My relationship with Him will continue to be so much more as I continue to invest and learn more about what a full and complete relationship with Him looks like.

Right now, I'm learning about embracing the Lord as a *friend*. The Lord wants that relationship with each of us— He declared it in John 15:15. He *calls us friends*. He wants to be the One we invite into each moment, the One to whom we run for comfort, the One we process with, the One we laugh and cry with, and the One we trust so deeply. He is our Beloved, and we are His (Song of Solomon 6:3).

I know this to be true in my head, but there are times when I find it more challenging for that truth to sink into my heart. In these moments, I ask the Lord to help me to continue seeing Him as my friend. I ask Him to continue to reveal these truths to my heart. And I continue to look forward to the day when we will be able to share a meal, reminisce about all we've been through, and enjoy each other's presence. Truthfully, just because it may take a while to sink in does not mean it's complicated. It's actually quite a simple truth: Jesus Christ has *already* called me His friend. Now, it is my beautiful responsibility to abide in Him and learn to walk that truth out until the day I am reunited with my dearest Friend, and we share a meal together.

A Continual Investment

Inviting the Lord into each aspect of our day and our life is undoubtedly the foundation. Still, we build on that foundation by investing time into relationship—a friendship—with Him. The Lord wants to invest in time with us—time that we choose to spend with Him above something or someone else. When we are faithful to give that quality time to the Lord, I believe He is faithful to meet us in it. Jeremiah 29:12–13 says,

> "'Then you will call upon Me and come and pray to Me, and I will listen to you. You will seek Me and find Me when you search for Me with all your heart'" (NASB).

Rest in the confidence that the Lord deeply desires relationship with you and wants to commune with you in a way you best connect with Him.

I think many of us have subconsciously built this idea of investing in relationship with the Lord into a complicated formula that we must follow to grow and dive deeper. But I believe the Lord created us to find Him more simply, and in that simplicity, more deeply because we are connecting with Him in a way we best communicate. Take some time to discover how you best connect with the Lord and embrace that life-giving time. The Lord is ready and willing to listen to us, be found by us, spend quality time with us, and be friends with us—what a beautiful responsibility we now have to enjoy the process of inviting Him in and then cultivating that relationship.

In what way(s) can I practically take a step forward today to engage in quality time with the Lord?

_____

_____

_____

_____

Heavenly Father, I want to grow deeper in my relationship with You. Would You show me how I can best engage in relationship with You? Please increase a desire in my heart to spend time with You. Amen.

The Lord has created each
of us uniquely and wired us to
communicate in different ways.
Just as we communicate
differently with those around us,
the Lord communicates
differently and uniquely with
each of us.

chapter 3

Simply Loved...

I've been thinking about this chapter for a few days now, and I can't seem to get it out of my head. In an effort to be totally transparent, I must confess that I wasn't initially planning to write this chapter. But as I prayed more and more over this book, I felt deep in my spirit that we must first settle who we are for any of us to understand the simplest thing. We are deeply loved.

The simplest thing is truly that: a simple act. It's an invitation. There's no complicated way we have to say it, no hoops we need to jump through, and no deep cleaning that must be done before extending the invite. It's simple. It's straightforward. We extend this invitation once at the moment of salvation and then over and over again as we invest in relationship with the Father.

But I fear this invitation to relationship won't have its full impact unless we understand the heart of the One on the other side. Think about it: who in your life do you turn to when the going gets tough? When you need advice, comfort, or counsel? You turn to the people who have your best interests at heart. You turn to the people who care for you and want to see you succeed. You cannot listen to all of the voices in your life because there would be too many. You listen to the ones closest to you, the ones who love you, and the ones who care enough to point you in the right direction. You listen because you know you are loved by them.

We know we are loved by the people closest to us because we can audibly hear their words, feel their touch, and see their support. We can remember back to the times they have supported us in the past. We can trust them. Can I be honest? Sometimes it's more challenging to *know* the Lord's love.

Declaring His Promises of Love

Growing up in a Christian home, I learned to "put on my armor." This comes from Ephesians 6, where Paul talks about putting on the full armor of God. The final piece of armor that I prayed over myself was always to "take up the sword of the Spirit, which is the Word of God." For as long as I can remember, the sword of the Spirit has been my way of combatting depression, anxiety, fear, worry ... you name it. Even when the promises didn't *feel* true, I claimed them anyway. That was my weapon.

Even to this day, the Scriptures I pray immediately after taking up the sword of the Spirit are the ones declaring the Lord's love for me. I audaciously claim that I am the beloved of the Lord, that nothing can separate me from His love, and that His love for me is everlasting. I don't think I ever really pondered why these were the first verses I claimed; they just sort of came out.

My youth pastor growing up said once, "The more you pray something, the more it becomes a reality." He didn't mean it as a guarantee that if we prayed fervently for a million dollars, we would have it. He meant the change that would take place would be a change in our hearts. The more we prayed for joy, the more our hearts would shift to recognize life and beauty all around. The more we prayed for love, the more the Lord would soften our hearts toward those surrounding us. The more we prayed for peace, the more we would be filled with trust in the Lord and His faithfulness.

His Love Is Our Foundation

I think the Lord prompted my heart every time I "put on my armor" to declare His love as my fighting words because He knew I had to understand that before I could do anything else. If I am going to confidently extend an invitation to the Lord to come and do whatever He sees best in my life, I *have to* settle in my heart that He loves me with an overwhelming love. Only to this kind of love can I fearlessly surrender my life and my future.

I think it's easy to brush God's love aside for some of His other promises. Not in an intentionally forgetful or malicious way; I just think we tend to cling to other, more tangible promises. We need Him to stay true to His promise to be faithful, provide, give wisdom, or direct our paths. But every single one of these promises finds its roots in His love. It's because of His love that we can confidently claim each of these other promises. When we understand the sureness of His great love for us, we can know for certain that He will not turn back on His words to us.

God's Perspective

John 3:16 isn't the only time God declares His great love for us. Hang with me for a moment because I want to take some time to walk through a list of His declarations of love. I want us to read these words and allow them to soak into our parched souls. These words are truth. They're not just words on a page. These are personal words, declaring how the Father feels about each of us. When we understand and claim these truths, the invitation becomes so much easier to extend. When we know the depths of His love for us, we want to invite Him into each and every moment. With a love that great, I desperately want Him to do what He sees is best for me because I know He will never let me down. Read these verses as they were meant to be read: truths declared about our Father in His Word that we can claim as *promises*.

His love is everlasting ....

"'I have loved you, my people, with an everlasting love. With unfailing love, I have drawn you to myself.'" Jeremiah 31:3

His love is good and unfailing ....

"O Lord, you are so good, so ready to forgive, so full of unfailing love for all who ask for your help." Psalm 86:5

His love is steady and endless ....

"The Lord is compassionate and merciful, slow to get angry and filled with unfailing love." Psalm 103:8

His love is fresh each and every day ....

"The faithful love of the Lord never ends! His mercies never cease. Great is his faithfulness; his mercies begin afresh each morning." Lamentations 3:22–23

His love shelters and protects us ....

"How precious is your unfailing love, O God! All humanity finds shelter in the shadow of your wings." Psalm 36:7

His love catches us when we fall ....

"I cried out, 'I am slipping!' but your unfailing love, O Lord, supported me. When doubts filled my mind, your comfort gave me renewed hope and cheer." Psalm 94:18–19

His love is forgiving ....

Where is another God like you, who pardons the guilt of the remnant, overlooking the sins of his special people? You will not stay angry with your people forever, because you delight in showing unfailing love. Micah 7:18

His love sacrificed everything for us ....

"This is real love—not that we loved God, but that he loved us and sent his Son as a sacrifice to take away our sins." 1 John 4:10

We are His beloved ....

"I am my beloved's, and my beloved is mine." Song of Solomon 6:3 (NIV)

He loves us as a perfect Father ....

"See how very much our Father loves us, for he calls us his children, and that is what we are." 1 John 3:1

When all else falls away, His love stays strong ....

"'For the mountains may move and the hills disappear, but even then my faithful love for you will remain. My covenant of blessing will never be broken,' says the Lord, who has mercy on you." Isaiah 54:10

His love is too great for us to grasp ....

And may you have the power to understand, as all God's people should, how wide, how long, how high, and how deep his love is. May you experience the love of Christ, though it is too great to understand fully. Then you will be made complete with all the fullness of life and power that comes from God. Ephesians 3:18–19

Nothing can ever separate us from His love ....

And I am convinced that nothing can ever separate us from God's love. Neither death nor life, neither angels nor demons, neither our fears for today nor our worries about tomorrow—not even the powers of hell can separate us from God's love. No power in the sky above or in the earth below—indeed, nothing in all creation will ever be able to separate us from the love of God that is revealed in Christ Jesus our Lord. Romans 8:38–39

These Scriptures barely scratch the surface. They're merely a drop in the ocean.

Our Perspective

Sometimes I repeat these promises out of routine. Because, if I'm being honest, sometimes it is challenging to feel the Lord's love. I cannot see Him with my physical eyes, I cannot hear His audible voice, and I cannot feel the warmth of a hug from Him. On days when He seems distant, it is so hard to feel His love. But these robotic declarations on the days when I barely hear the words coming out of my own mouth are not to change His heart. His heart is constant. C. S. Lewis said, "Though our feelings come and go, God's love for us does not" (*Mere Christianity*). These declarations on the days when I'm not feeling it are meant to change *my* heart. The more I pray something, the more that it becomes a reality. This is why these Scriptures are my fighting words.

Think of the person in this world who loves you most. Maybe it's a family member, spouse, or friend. Picture that person. Think about the times they have come through for you in the past. Think about the way you instinctively grab your phone to talk with them—celebrating the joys and mourning the tragedies. Think about how you know without a shadow of a doubt that they have your back, they want your best, and they will do whatever is in their power to take care of you.

The Lord loves you more.

And if you've never experienced that kind of love, know that the Lord longs to give it to you. His love is far beyond any human expression of love we will ever encounter. Whether you return the feelings or not, He loves you more. Whether you've been far from Him your whole life, He loves you more. Whether you've followed Him then turned your back on Him, He loves you more. He will always love you more.

His Love Does Not Depend on Us

It's so easy to think His love falters or wanes when we've done something contrary to His will. It makes sense in our minds because that's how we tend to operate as humans. When someone does something particularly hurtful, rejects us, turns their backs on us, or fails to invest in relationship with us, our love can feel strained. Naturally, we extend this image to the Lord's love for us.

We have trouble believing deep down that we are the beloved of the Lord when we have rejected Him, walked in sin, or just haven't really invested in relationship with Him in months. I understand. But, my friends, what makes us think we are the exception to His rule?

Abraham was fearful, lied, and allowed his wife, Sarah (who, by the way, laughed in the face of God's promises), to be put in a situation where she may have been forced into adultery to save his own life. God loved him and called him faithful, blessed, and the father of many nations.

Jacob was a liar and a deceiver. And he was greedy! He

stole blessings from his older brother and then ran away from his home. The Lord loved him and gave him a new name: Israel.

David ignored some of his responsibilities, committed adultery, got a married woman pregnant, and had her husband killed to cover up his affair. God loved him through it all, and he is called a man after God's own heart.

Peter denied that he even knew Christ. He denied it three separate times even though he swore to Jesus that he would die with Him. Jesus still loved him enough to *die for him*, and He said Peter was the rock upon which He would build His Church.

Paul was a first-hand party to the persecution and murder of Christians. It took an appearance from Jesus Himself to change Paul's mind. God loved him and called him to share the message of Jesus to the Gentiles. The Apostle Paul wrote a confirmed 13 books of the New Testament and was one of the gospel's greatest evangelists.

I remind us of all these people in the Bible not to condone any of their actions or excuse what they did because "God loved them anyway." I remind us of these people because, despite everything they did to deliberately hurt the Father, He welcomed them back with open arms. His love for them never faltered for a moment. His love for me has never faltered. His love for *you* has never faltered. And if I think that it has, then I have to stop myself and ask why on earth would little old me be the exception to His rule? If He has made promises about His unfailing love and they've proven true for all of humanity, why would I be any different? I've made my mistakes, but His love is always there. And when I return to Him, He embraces me like a loving Father.

The Heart of Our Father
It's like the parable of the prodigal son in Luke 15. The son

told his father that he wanted his inheritance now (which, in essence, told the father that he wished he was dead). He took the inheritance and wasted it on shameful living. In the end, when he looks around, he realizes that he has reached rock bottom. The only way out would be to return to his father and beg his forgiveness.

As he returns home, we read in Luke 15:20 that while he was "still a long way off, his father saw him." What does that tell us? While the son had insulted his father, left his home, and lived a truly soiled life, his place in his father's heart was unchanged. His father waited and watched for the return of his son. The instant he saw him on the horizon, he was filled with compassion, ran to meet him, and threw his arms around him to welcome him home.

This is how our Father loves us. He eagerly watches and waits for us to return. And the moment He sees us coming back, He runs to us and welcomes us with open arms. At that moment of repentance, there is no shame over what's been done. There is only unconditional love. There will only ever be unconditional love. That's just how our Father is.

Settling His Love in Our Hearts

This is the truth that will never fail. And this is the truth that the enemy will always want us to doubt the most. I think that's why the simple truth of God's love is sometimes the hardest for us to grasp. Because once this truth ultimately settles in our hearts, our faith to believe the rest of His promises will be unshakeable. That's why those declarations of His love despite my feelings are my fighting words. That's why these Scriptures pour out of my heart when I take up the sword of the Spirit.

My friends, before we take one more step on this journey of discovering the simplest thing, we must settle this truth in our hearts: we are the beloved of the

Most High God. His love for us is everlasting, unfailing, and sure. His love is sacrificial, perfect, forgiving, and steadfast. His love surpasses any human love we have ever experienced. And out of His love flows every other promise He has made to us. When we extend the invitation for Him to come into a moment, we are inviting the very Lover of our souls to come and do what He sees best. No one cares more for our future than He. That exact sentence should cause our faith to burst! If we believe—not just in our minds but truly settle in our hearts and spirits—what Scripture says, then we can trust that He will take care of us.

This truth is simple: God loves us, no matter what. And He's *already* given us the full measure of His love! But what a difficult truth to grasp. Can I propose a thought? To fully understand this truth, we must extend an invitation. He loves us so much that He wants to help us fully understand His love. When His love is too great to fully understand or grasp completely, all we need to do is invite Him in to *reveal* His love to us in a new way. It's His greatest pleasure to help us understand the vastness of His love for us. Just as we read Paul's prayer for the church in Ephesians 3:18 earlier, so we can pray for ourselves: "Father, would we have the power to understand, as all God's people should, how wide, how long, how high, and how deep is Your love for us."

> 1 John 5:14–15 says, "And we are confident that He hears us whenever we ask for anything that pleases Him. And since we know He hears us when we make our requests, we also know that He will give us what we ask for."

Friends, it pleases the heart of the Father when we ask Him for His help to understand His great love for us. As we continue to invite Him in to deepen our understanding of His great love, our love and faith continue to grow, causing us to want to continue to extend the invitation. We've entered a cycle—a cycle of asking for more understanding of His love, receiving more understanding of His love, and wanting to ask for more of it all over again. I'd say our loving God is pretty smart.

Which Scripture speaks most to my heart about God's love for me? Or which Scripture am I having the hardest time believing about God's love for me?

_____

_____

_____

_____

I choose to claim this promise and believe it as the Father's declaration of love toward me.

Heavenly Father, thank You for Your great love for me. Would You give me a deeper understanding of Your love for me today? Amen.

When we understand
the sureness of His great
love for us, we can
know for certain that
He will not turn back on
His words to us.

chapter 4

Simply Not About Feelings...

Life seems to be utterly full of ups and downs. It's never quite satisfied with one particular season, schedule, or routine, and you never really know how long it will be before it decides to change again. Some seasons drag on a bit longer than we would like, and others seem to fly by before we get the chance to settle in and breathe deeply.

In Case You Forgot, Life Can Be Crazy

Growing up, I spent almost every weekend at a horse show. And every morning in between, I was up early before the sun got hot to train with my horse. We worked hard, and we loved competing. Show days were always long and required a lot of preparation. They'd start before dawn with a bath for my two-ton horse and end with cramped legs after spending all day in the saddle. But between you and me, there is no better feeling than sitting on top of a horse on a hot summer day. There's just something about the sense of freedom mixed with the partnership between you and such a powerful animal that's hard to beat, in my opinion.

One particular show day took place mid-May in Colorado. We hadn't lived in the Sunshine State very long, but we'd been warned about the crazy spring weather

Colorado had to offer. We're from the Midwest. How much more "crazy" can it really get? Allow me to explain.

We arrived at the show bright and early. I was out in a tank top sweating under the sun as I unloaded my horse and saddled her up for a warm-up before the competition started. About halfway into the morning, the clouds came. It began to sprinkle. Then came the pouring rain. After a few minutes, the rain turned to hail and sleet. What next? You guessed it! Snow. It snowed for about an hour before the sun peaked out again, and I was back in my tank top. I think I even got a sunburn that day. When people say you can see all four seasons in one day in Colorado, they're telling the truth. I've lived in a couple of other states since Colorado, and everyone there tries to tell me that their weather is crazy. Listen, until you've lived in Colorado in the spring, you just don't understand.

I think sometimes life can be much like the weather that spring day at the horse show. It's unpredictable, it changes, and sometimes those changes happen faster than you're able to take them in. One minute the sun is shining, and before your sunscreen has the chance to dry, you're running for cover to avoid being pelted by golf ball–sized hail. You slip on some snow along the way, and by the time you reach shelter, the sun's back out again. It's almost as though life feels like a heartbeat at times—how fitting. Up, down, rest. Up, down, rest. Up, down, rest.

While life certainly contains ups, downs, and rests, it by no means feels the need to follow any particular order. Sometimes it's down, up, down, rest. Other times it's up, rest, up, rest, plummet back down again. I understand the need for these rhythmic changes, but wouldn't it be so much simpler if life followed at least some sort of predictable pattern? In my mind, predictability is comforting and reliable.

But how many of us know life rarely fits this picture?

More often than not, it's a spring day in Colorado. It can be hectic and pleasant, refreshing and draining. And I think this relentless beating—the ups, the downs, the periodic rests—is what presses us closer to the Lord. It forces us to simply hang onto Him for the ride and sometimes, as it may seem, for dear life. When life flatlines, I'm left feeling lifeless and without much need to hang onto the Lord.

Feelings Can Be Even Crazier

Seasons of life are fickle, and truthfully, so are my feelings. I find myself riding the roller-coaster of ups and downs, and sometimes it seems like a long journey before there is a rest. To be honest, lately, my life has felt like a lot of ups and downs without much rest. The heartbeat rhythm of my life feels more irregular and somewhat like I'm in the middle of running a marathon. It is unbelievably easy to fall into the trap of feeling overwhelmed by it all.

In these moments, I find myself losing sight of the beauty of simplicity in my relationship with the Lord. Yet it is in these exact moments when the simplicity is so profound. Life may be overwhelming and splitting at the seams, but my relationship with the Lord still rests upon that one invitation. I must consciously remember to take a step back and invite the Lord into the ups, downs, and rests in my life. I remind myself that He is the One from whom I draw my strength.

C. S. Lewis is one of my favorite authors. This man knew a thing or two about changing circumstances—his life regularly flew back and forth between up and down. From fighting in wars to converting from atheism to Christianity and remarkable literary successes to losing his wife to ill- ness, he knew what it felt like to experience the highest highs and the lowest lows. He wrote once, "Faith ... is the art of holding on to things ... in spite of your changing moods" (*Mere Christianity*). Allow that to sink in for a moment.

The biggest step of faith is extending that one simple invitation and believing it will be accepted. And can I let you in on a little secret? We have promise after promise that the invitation will be accepted—every single time.

When we get so consumed in our circumstances and can't see the forest for the trees, it is easy to feel weak and insufficient. It is easy to wonder where the Lord is in those moments. But let me tell you, He has never left. Scripture is full of promises that the Lord will be right by our sides, He is with us always, and He will never leave or forsake us. Verses like Matthew 28:20, Deuteronomy 31:6, Deuteronomy 31:8, Joshua 1:9, 1 Chronicles 28:20, and Isaiah 41:10, among many others, all proclaim the message very pointedly. He never leaves, He always hears, and His love is constant.

Faith is the art of holding on to things in spite of your changing moods and circumstances. Regardless of what my feelings or circumstances tell me in a given moment, I must hold on to the assurance that if I invite the Lord in, He will always come. No exceptions. That, my friends, is faith. Because His truth and His promises are more real than anything this world could ever tell us, show us, or make us feel.

But what about the times when we call out to the Lord, and we don't hear an answer? What about the moments we invite Him in but still can't seem to feel Him or see Him at work? Or the moments when we're begging for just a touch of encouragement or small blessing from the Lord to help us see the light at the end of the tunnel, and nothing comes? What good does it do to invite Him in if we have to wonder if He's *really* even there, right? He said He would be my Source and Strength, but it feels a bit like He's failing on His promises. Don't be so shocked. I'm sure you yourself have had some of those same thoughts in your own moments of weakness.

C. S. Lewis also had something to say about this in *Till We Have Faces*: "I know now, Lord, why You utter no answer.

You are Yourself the answer. Before Your face, questions die away. What other answer would suffice?" Sometimes we cannot feel Him. Sometimes we don't receive the answer we thought we needed. It's because He is the answer. It's because our hearts soften and our relationships deepen when we choose to seek Him, even in the silence. He may not utter an answer, but He is still there. His presence has never lifted, and before Him, all questions fade away. He is present, and He is our sufficient answer.

Even When We Can't Feel Him

I read once about a dream a woman had in which she saw three women kneeling and praying. Then she saw the Lord in the dream walk up to the three women. At the first woman, He stopped and lavished love on her, encouraged her, and spoke sweetly to her. At the second woman, He stopped, smiled at her, and put His hand on her shoulder. As He approached the third woman, He barely glanced at her and kept walking by.

The woman having the dream thought to herself: *He obviously loves the first one, the second one He seemed pleased with, but the third one! I wonder what she must have done to upset the Lord so that He wouldn't even stop?*

Then the Lord appeared to the woman having the dream and said she had it all wrong. He said, "I love each of these women equally and hear all of their prayers. The first woman is new to My love and needs constant affirmation and support from Me to keep her faith strong. The second woman I trust to continue to follow Me with a little encouragement. But the third woman! I trust her so fully to follow Me whether or not she *feels* My love and encouragement."

Let me be very honest with you: I know what it feels like to wake up in the morning, make my cup of coffee, search the Scriptures, and not feel anything resonate deeply.

I know what it feels like to ask the Lord for answers and seemingly get silence as my response. I know what it feels like to not *feel* the Lord. And then the feelings of guilt and fear sneak in: have I done something to keep the Lord from loving me? Does He hear my prayers? Is there something I need to do for Him to answer me? Is He angry with me? Does He care about all that I am going through and seeking Him about? Oh, my friends, please listen closely: our feelings do not determine His presence.

Our Efforts Won't Fix Our Relationship with the Lord

When we do not instantly feel or hear Him, we can be tempted to take the responsibility of the relationship on our own shoulders. We plan, we work, and we strive. When we take on this responsibility and add "Fix relationship with the Lord" to our growing to-do list, we are pulled out of simplicity. For what is begun by *our* efforts must be maintained by *our* efforts. We are no longer taking the simple step to abide in Him and invite Him in to do His work. We take on the mantle of complication, and despite our many efforts, we find ourselves drifting further and further from intimacy with the Father.

Simplicity does not equate to ease. Sometimes the simplest thing of inviting the Lord in and abiding in Him is the most challenging choice we will make, especially when we don't feel Him. Yet when we choose the sometimes-difficult option of resting in Him, we can rest assured that He is here and He is moving, even when we can't *feel* it. He has promised when we pray, He will listen (Jeremiah 29:12), His presence will never leave us (Matthew 28:20), and nothing on earth or under the earth could ever separate us from His love (Romans 8:38–39). His love is constant, and His presence is eternal—whether we feel and see it or not. John

Bevere explores this idea deeply in his book, *God, Where Are You?!*. He writes that God will never remove His presence from us—that is scriptural. But He will remove His *felt* presence from us and even lead us into seasons of wilderness to draw us closer to Him, equip us for change, and prepare us for what He has in the future.

Following Is Not About Feelings

Truthfully, I am inclined to believe that following the Lord when we don't noticeably feel His presence or see His hands working is even a more pure form of faith. Think about it: it is much easier to have faith and follow the Lord when it's easy—when we feel His presence daily, when we see His hand at work, and when we clearly hear His voice. But the walk to which we are called was never meant to be comfortable all of the time. How can our faith ever stretch and grow if we are never put in situations where our faith must be stretched and grown? Hebrews 11:1 gives us this definition of faith: faith is the substance of things hoped for, the evidence of things *not* seen. Talk about stretching! We're called to a life of hoping for things that we cannot even see. We are called to take up our crosses and follow Him (Luke 9:23). Some of the steps on our journey are meant to be laborious, heavy, and determined strides of faith. The key is that we were never intended to take those steps alone. His presence is there, regardless of our feelings.

I love the story of the footprints in the sand—old as it may be—because I think it shows the Lord's presence on our journeys in such a tangible way. It goes like this: *A man once had a dream where he was walking along the beach with the Lord. His walk symbolized his life, and when he got near the end, he looked back at the way they had come. He noticed several places where there were two sets of footprints—one for him and one for the Lord. But there were also many places where he saw only one set of footprints. This troubled the man greatly because he noticed these breaks came at the lowest and most difficult points in his walk. He questioned the Lord, "Lord, You said that if I followed You, You would walk with me all of the days of my life. Yet looking back, I see only one set of footprints in the most difficult places of my life. Why would You break Your promise and leave me—especially then?" The Lord replied, "My precious son, I love you, and I would never leave you. I walked with you always. The places where you see only one set of footprints—the places where your suffering and trials were the greatest—it was then that I carried you."*

What a beautiful picture of the Father's love. He honors His promises, He is always our answer, He never leaves us, and in fact, He often carries us when we do not have the strength to walk on our own—whether we feel it or not. The ups and downs of life will never change. Sometimes the weather will be crazy. There will always be joy-filled seasons, seasons of change, seasons of grace, and seasons of grief. The only constant through each of those seasons will be the presence of the Lord, the promise that He will never leave our sides, and the hope that He is working on our behalf.

He Is Enough

A couple of weeks ago, I was reading the Psalms, and the Lord spoke to my heart and challenged me through Psalm 16:11: "You will show me the way of life, granting me the joy of your presence and the pleasures of living with you forever."

As I read that, a series of questions rushed through my mind ....

What if this season I'm in—or a season I most dread—
never ends?
What if life by my standards never gets better?
What if I keep going down, and there's never an up or a rest?
In the times when I feel most alone, will the knowledge of His
presence, regardless of what my feelings tell me, be enough to
bring me real and lasting joy?
Will the future hope and pleasure of living with Him for
eternity be enough to sustain me?

I am still wrestling and challenging myself with these questions, but the one thing that I must continue to return to is the simple and *indisputable fact* that my feelings do not dictate the Lord's presence in my life. Even when the seasons of life are fickle, changing rapidly from sun to snow, He is right by my side. Even in my loneliest and longest seasons, I am simply not alone. Even when I cannot feel Him, He accepts my invitation every single time I extend it to Him. He carries me, and from Him, I draw my strength. The knowledge of His presence is enough to bring me joy, and I cling to the hope of living with Him forever—that is my life sustenance.

What feelings am I experiencing right now that may be contrary to God's truth?

_____

_____

_____

_____

Take a minute to pause and reflect on the feelings you just wrote down.

Heavenly Father, thank You for being constant despite my changing feelings. Would You help me recognize when what I feel is contrary to Your truth? And by the power of Your Holy Spirit, help my feelings match up with the truth. Amen.

**Our feelings
do not
determine
His presence.**

chapter 5

Simply with His Help…

———

As the Lord has been resonating the truth of His presence with me, there is one key lesson I have learned—and am truthfully still learning—in my walk with Christ that I wish I would have learned so much earlier. Maybe it was for lack of being taught, or maybe it was for lack of my understanding, but I didn't begin to recognize and grasp this vital truth until just a couple of years ago.

Track with me for a moment, if you will. In our everyday lives, we hear that we need to trust in the Lord in all circumstances, live lives full of the joy of the Lord, and surrender to Him in all things. Some days, these commands seem relatively simple and don't require a lot of effort to put into practice. Other days—most days, if I'm being honest—I'm afraid to trust the Lord, not because I believe He won't take care of me, but rather I worry where His plan will lead. C. S. Lewis put it well when he said, "We are not necessarily doubting that God will do the best for us; we are wondering how painful the best will turn out to be" (*Letters to An American Lady*).

My decision to trust can often be difficult. Similarly, choosing the joy of the Lord often fights against every natural, fleshly inclination to fall into the comfortable embrace of sadness, irritability, or apathy. It is work to choose joy when life around me screams otherwise. And surrendering?

Remember, I love a good plan, and the thought that my beautiful plan may not come to fruition? Wow. That is a tough pill to swallow. These and more are everyday battles I face, and I'd be inclined to say you're not being one hundred percent honest if you claimed you didn't encounter them, too.

Now you're probably wondering why I deviated so far from making my original point with all of these friendly reminders of our struggles and inadequacies as if we'd forgotten they exist. Well, these are struggles we face on a daily, if not minute-by-minute, basis. But the key lesson that rocked my world and my faith is we were never meant to struggle alone. I know what you must be thinking: you just now figured this out? But hang with me for a minute. So often, we believe *we must* figure out how to live lives of joy despite our circumstances. We think it is *our job* to let go of our plans and surrender to the Lord. We believe it is *our responsibility* to trust always in the Lord. Now, we can make the weight of these decisions all fall solely on our shoulders, but I guarantee you we will fail more than we succeed because these actions require a supernatural strength we simply do not possess. Remember? What we begin in our own strength must be maintained by our own strength. Or, we can invite the Lord in to do what He does best.

He Helps Us in Our Weaknesses

In my reading one day, I stumbled across Romans 8:26, and it was like my eyes were opened to the significance of this Scripture:

"In the same way, the Spirit helps us in our weaknesses" (NIV).

The preceding verses in Romans 8 talk about the hope we

have as we wait for the fulfillment of our adoption in Christ and our redeemed lives. I would imagine when we reach the day of fulfillment of our adoption in Christ, and our lives are wholly redeemed and restored from our natural state of sin, we won't have trouble choosing joy, trusting the Father, or surrendering. But the Lord knows we are not there yet, which is why verse 26 is such a beautiful declaration: the Spirit *helps* us in our weaknesses. This is one of the jobs of the Spirit! One we do not embrace to its fullest potential.

Andrew Murray wrote a powerful book on one of my daily struggles: surrender. In his work *Absolute Surrender*, he writes,

> God does not ask you to give the perfect surrender in your strength, or by the power of your will; God is willing to work it in you. Do we not read, 'It is God who works in you both to will and to do for His good pleasure' (Philippians 2:13)? ... He will conquer what is evil and work what is well-pleasing in His blessed sight. God, Himself will work it in you.

> *The Spirit helps us in our weaknesses.*
> *It is God who works in us to will and do for His good pleasure.*
> *God, Himself will work it in you.*

Let the truth of that sink in for a moment. I am weak in so many areas. I feel overwhelmed and tired; I have to resist the urge to take control; I struggle with knowing the right path to take; I long for deep peace; and sometimes, I struggle with even having the faith to believe God will work out everything according to His perfect plan. But I take the deepest comfort in knowing that in my weaknesses, He is made strong. His strength is best displayed when I acknowledge my weakness before Him and invite Him into those places. I don't always feel an immediate shift, but I know I have taken the weight off my weak shoulders and placed it in His steady and unwavering grasp. It is still our responsibility to cooperate with the work the Holy Spirit is doing in our hearts, but the burden is no longer ours to bear alone. We have invited the Holy Spirit to do one of the jobs He does best: helping us in our weaknesses.

The simple yet profound act of inviting Him into our weaknesses also becomes an opportunity for the Lord to prove to us that He is a faithful God. Think about it: if we only ever took control, charged ahead, and plowed our own paths, never waiting for the Lord to direct or move, how could God display His faithfulness?

The faithfulness of the Lord is multifaceted. He is faithful to forgive, love, protect, correct, make right, restore, comfort ... we need only invite Him to be those things and rest as He accomplishes them. He is able. He delights when we cry out to Him in our weaknesses; for in our weakness, He is made strong. And each time we are weak or in need physically, mentally, emotionally, or spiritually and He proves Himself faithful, our trust in His faithfulness grows. If we never lacked anything, the Lord wouldn't be able to prove Himself faithful in our lives. We would be living life out of our own strength, accomplishment, wisdom, strategy, and intuition, instead of relying on the Lord to supernaturally supply all of our needs ... especially in our weakest moments.

Because We Are Weak

Can I be very candid? As I write tonight, I feel tired. I feel a little discouraged and overwhelmed by life right now. All day, I had been looking forward to settling in and doing a little writing, but as the day wore on, more things kept coming up, chipping away at my enthusiasm and leaving me a little more discouraged and overwhelmed.

As I sit here in the light of my lamp under a cable-knit blanket, I feel a little small. You know those days? When life hits a few times, and what's left feels slightly shrunken and depleted—weak? This has been one of those days. And as I sat down to write, I found myself asking the Lord if I even should write tonight. Should I write when I don't feel like I have anything to give? Is it pointless to circle a topic, trying to find the right words to say? Should I just rest tonight and try again tomorrow? Am I even qualified to share with others when I feel this way? It somehow felt wrong for me to sit and write words of encouragement when I felt broken and weary. But very quickly and very quietly, I felt the Lord whisper He wanted me to write. Very specifically, He wanted me to write *because* I did not feel as though I had much to give.

As I began to settle this in my heart, I remembered a recent revelation I had during my morning Bible reading. I was reading Matthew 14, and the first part of the chapter gives the account of John the Baptist's death. John the Baptist wasn't just another character in the Bible—he was Jesus' cousin, the one who went before Jesus to prepare Israel for His coming, and the one who baptized Jesus at the start of His ministry. I imagine that John the Baptist was a life-giving, iron-sharpening-iron man in Jesus' life. A true friend. While Jesus knew John the Baptist had fulfilled his calling on the earth and was now glorified with the Father, He was still fully man and felt the depth of that loss. He grieved.

In my own season of grief, I felt weak, weary, and worn. I wanted to retreat. And Jesus did just that—Matthew 14:13 says Jesus withdrew privately to go to a solitary place to be alone. But what happened? Matthew 14:14 says the crowds followed Him. And not to comfort Him or support Him in His time of need; no, they came for what He could do for them.

The following verses tell us Jesus had compassion for all

of these people and took the time to heal their sick. I must confess that I don't think I would have been as gracious as Jesus was. When I was grieving, I wanted people to surround me to support me. It was extremely difficult to find the energy to pour out to others. But Jesus poured out to the crowds all day, and by the time evening came, the people were hungry. Five thousand people were hungry, to be exact. Jesus blessed the five loaves and two fish collected by the disciples, fed all five thousand people, and had twelve baskets of bread left over.

This was one of the most well-known miracles of Jesus—the *only* miracle recorded in all four of the Gospels. And this miracle took place on the same day Jesus received some of the most grievous news of His ministry. What if Jesus had said to the people that He wanted to be alone to grieve? What if He said He felt too broken and weary to minister? On this day of all days, I think Jesus could have said He didn't have the energy to pour out. But instead, Jesus chose to abide in the strength and grace of the Father and have compassion on the people. This act of obedience to minister even in His brokenness set the stage for one of Jesus' greatest miracles to display the ultimate provision of God. And it serves as an amazing example for us now. Even on our weakest days, we are not disqualified from ministry. Those are days His power is made perfect in our weakness.

The more I study Scripture, the more I realize the Lord loves to use people who feel weak, small, broken, or insignificant. What a counter-cultural approach. Often, I think we subconsciously believe that it would do harm if we attempt to minister or pour out while we feel broken. We feel overwhelmed by the demands of life, we are consumed by grief, or we feel small and insignificant, and then we think we have little to give. Or perhaps we feel disqualified by our weaknesses and inadequacies. And if we were ministering out of *our own strength*, then we would be right! We would have very little—if anything—to give. This is why I think the Lord loves to use people who know they have little to offer on their own, because they must draw from His strength to succeed. In those people, His power is so blatantly obvious.

Our Weakness Highlights His Strength

I love the story of Gideon. In Gideon's story, an angel of the Lord appears to Gideon and greets him with: "The Lord is with you, mighty warrior," and goes on to say, "Go in the strength you have and save Israel out of Midian's hand. Am I not sending you?" (Judges 6:12, 14). Gideon doesn't seem to hear the label the angel (of the Lord) gives him; instead, he responds to the angel by describing himself as part of the weakest clan in Manasseh and as the least in his family. He expresses to the angel that he feels weak, small, broken, and insignificant. By all of the world's standards, I don't think Gideon was wrong to feel weak and insignificant—it sounds like he genuinely was.

I'm going to pause for a moment here and reflect on this fact: the truth of the world around him said that Gideon was weak and insignificant. Sometimes, the world around us leaves us feeling vulnerable, weary, broken, and unimportant. There may be people in your life who you are regularly forced to encounter that put you down, you may have faced significant loss, or you may be walking through transition, and all of life feels unstable. Sometimes, our worlds do indeed leave us feeling small, broken, and weary. This was the case with Gideon—his world left him feeling weak, small, and insignificant. But what he saw as a hindrance—as a *disqualifier*—God saw as an opportunity to display His greatness.

Let's go back to the angel's commission: "Go *in the strength you have* and save Israel ... Am I not sending you?" The Lord was well aware of the strength Gideon had, and He knew Gideon would answer out of his perceived inadequacy. This is why the Lord responds to Gideon's hesitations immediately with: "I will be with you." What we see as a disqualifier, God sees as an opportunity to display His greatness. He will be with us.

If you know the ending to Gideon's story, not only does God choose a small and seemingly insignificant man to lead His army to victory, but He shrinks this army down from twenty-two thousand to three hundred. Talk about *small* and *insignificant*. The Lord wanted to wipe away every single ounce of human strength in this story and emphasize the weakness of these men, so the only possible explanation for victory would be the strength of the Lord. I have never heard anyone reflect on Gideon's story and talk about the strength of Gideon. I have only ever heard reflections in awe and wonder about the unmatched *strength of the Lord*. And I'm learning that this is the reflection the Lord wants others to have on our lives, as well.

We will all face days when we feel weak, inadequate, and unprepared for the task ahead of us, leaving us wondering if we should even proceed. Billy Graham was arguably one of the greatest ministers and evangelists to walk the earth. It's estimated that over two million people came to know the Lord through his preaching. Prior to one of Mr. Graham's events, he said:

> I do not know that I have ever felt more inadequate
> and totally unprepared for a mission. As I think over
> the possibility for messages, I realize how shallow
> and weak my presentations are. In fact, I was so

overwhelmed with my unpreparedness that I almost decided to cancel my appearance, but because plans have gone so far perhaps it is best to go through with it. … However, it is my prayer that I shall come in the demonstration and power of the Holy Spirit.

Instead of choosing to give in to his feelings of weakness and inadequacy, he decided to press into the strength and power of the Holy Spirit. I wonder if Billy Graham had chosen to give in each time he felt unqualified, there would be fewer people who now know the strength of the Lord in their own lives. He decided to press into the Lord in his weakness, and the Lord was unquestionably given glory.

There will always be days when this world's ups and downs leave us feeling a little weary and deflated. And there will be days when we do not *feel* the presence of the Lord in our lives. But we must never let our feelings on those days keep us from the simple and most powerful act of pressing into what the Lord has called us to do. When we are most empty, we are most available to be filled with the Holy Spirit. What we may see as disqualifiers in our lives to minister, the Lord sees as opportunities to display His strength and glory. When I was in a season of life where I felt particularly weak, a friend said to me that the Lord does not just want to give me strength; He wants to *be* my strength.

There will indeed be moments ahead when we feel weak, inadequate, and broken, but in these moments, we have to return to the Lord, invite Him in, and ask Him to *be* our strength. This act is simple but requires great faith when we still feel weary. Psalm 118:14 says that the Lord is our strength and our salvation. The Lord wants to be our strength, He wants to shine through us with His glory, and He does it best when we surrender to Him and allow His power to work through us.

When we feel weak and weary, left with little strength, the promise of the Lord from the story of Gideon says that His strength will be sufficient, and it will be for His glory. When all of life is overwhelming, our relationship with the Lord still hinges on the simplest thing. Every moment of every day—the moments when we feel adequate and the moments when we feel inadequate—let us invite Him in and then watch as we move forward simply with His help. Let it become our prayer that when we are weak, then He is strong; may we hope that when people look on at our lives, they see not our strength but the glory of the Lord and His faithfulness in our lives. What a simple, stretching, and powerful truth.

In what area do I feel weak today and need to invite the Holy Spirit to be my strength?

_____

_____

_____

_____

Heavenly Father, thank You for the promise that Your Holy Spirit helps me when I feel weak. Today, I bring You into (fill in the blank). Would You be my strength in this area? Amen.

The simple yet profound act of inviting Him into our weaknesses also becomes an opportunity for the Lord to prove to us that He is a faithful God.

chapter 6

Simply Growing…

I have decided that Psalm 27 is close to the top of my list of favorite Psalms. This chapter is packed full of simple pleas from the heart of David to remain close to the heart of the Father. I was reading it recently and was reminded once again that trusting the Lord brings the deepest possible comfort. One verse in particular stood out to me, however, in a way it had not before. In Psalm 27:14, David writes,

> "Wait patiently for the Lord. Be brave and courageous. Yes, wait patiently for the Lord."

I am in a season of waiting, myself, so I think I tend to notice more when Scripture talks about waiting. I found it interesting that tucked in between two exhortations to wait for the Lord was the call to be brave and courageous. Coincidence? I don't think so.

Waiting Is a Tool in the Hand of the Father

The word "wait," when examined in the context of *waiting on* someone, literally means to stay where one is or delay action until that someone arrives or is ready. David tells us to be brave and courageous as we stay where we are until the Lord arrives or is ready.

On our journey of embracing the simplest thing, we are often called to wait. As we seek to abide in the Father and invite Him in as the foundation of our relationship, sometimes He draws us into a season of waiting. As we invite Him in to move and have His way in our hearts, sometimes He asks us to wait upon Him because He is working behind the scenes. Other times, waiting is a precious tool in the hand of the Father to draw our hearts ever closer to His. Whatever the reason, we can invite Him in and rest in confidence that He is, in fact, working.

If you've ever had to be in one of these seasons of waiting, then you know it often takes far more courage to stay exactly where you are instead of accomplishing tasks that push you closer to your goal. When you are in a "doing" stage, you are given the opportunity to move forward, complete tasks, and see change. When you are in a waiting stage, you must be still and know that He is God, stay where you are until the Lord shows up or is ready, and resist the fear that you might be missing out on something you cannot see at the moment because you have been waiting.

Waiting Doesn't Mean Something Isn't Happening

Now let me be clear, I do not think that waiting patiently on the Lord means sitting around and twiddling our thumbs. I believe the Lord can do absolutely anything, but we certainly make it difficult for Him to work in and through us when we sit around doing nothing. I don't know if you've tried, but it's pretty hard to turn a parked car. See my point? I believe waiting instead means being in a place of rest and remaining faithful to the season in which the Lord has placed us. As we pause in these seasons, we wait for the next thing to which the Lord is calling us. We've got the car on and in gear, but we have our foot on the brake waiting for the Navigator's signal as He finalizes our directions. We remain in the season in which He has placed us until He is ready for us to move into the next season. My pastor always said, "If you don't know the next step you're supposed to take, then just do the last thing the Lord told you to do until He tells you something different."

Waiting Can Cultivate Fertile Soil

Often these seasons of waiting are designed by the Master Creator to be seasons of cultivation and growth. Some time ago, I was rereading Mark 4, where Jesus tells the parable of the sower. In this parable, a farmer went out to plant his seed. In Jesus' day, crops weren't grown in neat rows; instead, a farmer had a better chance of yielding a great harvest if he scattered much seed as he went through his fields. However, as the farmer throws fistfuls of seed out, not all of it would fall in the fields. Some of the seeds would land along the path, and as Jesus said, the birds would come and eat it. Some of the seeds would fall on the rocky ground where there was little soil. The seed would spring up quickly but would just as quickly be scorched by the sun and wither away because the soil was too shallow. Some of the seeds would fall amongst the thorns and would soon be choked by the weeds, unable to produce grain. But some of the seeds would fall on good soil. These seeds would thrive and grow, yielding a crop up to a hundred times over.

Jesus goes on in the next several verses of Mark 4 to explain this parable. The farmer is sowing the Word of God. Some people are like the soil of the seed tossed along the path. As soon as they hear it, the enemy of our soul comes and takes it away. Other people are like the rocky ground's soil—they receive the seed, but because it does not go deep down and develop roots, they soon forget it when trials or persecution come. Others are like the soil of the seed sown amongst the weeds and thorns—the worries of this life, distractions, and desires for other things quickly choke the Word. But those who are like the good soil hear the Word, accept it, and in time, produce an abundant and lasting crop.

I think we all hear this story and hope we're in the last category. We want our names counted among those who hear the Word of the Lord and produce a fruitful and lasting crop. We want the soil of our hearts to be rich and fertile, ready to accept what the Lord is speaking to us. We want the roots to thrive, go down deep, and spring up in vibrant new life. We desire lasting change in our hearts! Now, I hope I'm not the first to tell you (and I certainly won't be the last) that lasting change takes time and often requires waiting.

Cultivation Requires a Process

As I was thinking over this passage and talking with the Lord about what it looks like for the soil of my heart to be ready to receive the seed, I took a moment to reflect on the old-fashioned cultivation of soil. I'm originally from central Nebraska. I grew up in a farming community right outside of a town with a population of a little more than two thousand five hundred. My home was nestled in the middle of corn and soybean fields—I have a good understanding of traditional farming and know the work and preparation that goes into producing a good crop.

A farmer cannot merely buy a plot of land, walk onto the field, toss out some seed, and expect a bountiful return. He must wait and endure the process of preparation before the seed can ever even be planted. The most fertile soil is rich and watered. But the most significant piece that prepares the ground for planting—the primary factor that determines whether or not the farmer will yield a good crop—is the plowing or tilling of the fields in the proper season.

A good farmer knows that he must wait for the right time to prepare his fields for planting. He cannot prepare his fields and then attempt to plant his seeds in the frozen ground of winter. He also cannot cultivate the land and plant in the scorching heat of summer when the crops would dry up before the roots had a chance to go down deep. The farmer knows the season and time for the seed to be planted and patiently waits for that right time to produce an abundant harvest.

When the farmer has waited for the right time to plant, he drives his tractor through his fresh fields and cuts through the hard, dry topsoil with the blades. Churning the rich soil, he mixes the ground and creates a safe place for the seed to be planted. Often, the weather elements leave the previously untouched top layer of the soil depleted of nutrients and crusted over. I think if the seed were to be planted without the churning of the soil, it would be much like the seed that fell on the path—birds would come and eat it, or the wind would blow it away. Or many times, these fields are already overrun with grasses and weeds, and the seed would be choked out before it has the chance to produce a crop. Untouched soil is not the best to produce a harvest.

It is important to note that the farmer doesn't look at the soil in frustration and deem it worthless to yield his crop nor does he cower at the wait or grow weary of the process. Instead, he knows the rich soil that lies just beneath the surface, and he knows exactly how to get it ready to receive the seed which will bring him a great harvest. He is committed to that field and patiently waits because he knows the potential it holds.

I believe it is much the same way with our own hearts. Truthfully, our hearts are not always ready to receive the seed. Sometimes, the elements of life have left it depleted of nutrients and crusted over. Or perhaps, weeds of bitterness or fear have sprung up and taken over. But the Lord does not look at our hearts in these conditions with frustration or disgust; no, He looks at them full of anticipation because He sees the deep richness just waiting to be uncovered.

Our Father desires an invitation from us to come in and work because He sees the beautiful potential of an intimate and fulfilling relationship in our hearts. He, like the farmer, knows the great return that will come out of the soil once it has been made ready. So out of love, He churns the soil of our hearts. This process is often long and painful—old ground is broken through, old thoughts are challenged, old lies are uncovered, and old scars are reopened. This plowing is not being done to cause us harm; instead, the pain's purpose is to bring healing, wholeness, and growth. It prepares us to receive the seeds the Lord longs to plant in our hearts.

I don't mean for this to strike fear in your hearts or unearth feelings of anger or frustration that the Lord would do such a thing. Instead, I mean for it to inspire hope! We all face trials and struggles in life, we all go through seasons of pain, and we all experience times when our worlds feel unsteady. We long for the simplicity of abiding in Christ and growing out of a place of intimacy with Him, but we can't seem to find the good soil beneath the weathered and weed-covered surface. We want nothing more than to be brave and courageous as we wait upon the Lord, but we feel as though our hearts are being churned, broken, and plowed.

When these seasons of cultivation come, I believe it is because the Lord is preparing us for a seed He desires to plant in our hearts. And I firmly believe that we have two distinct choices when we find ourselves in these situations. We could allow this brokenness to make us bitter, angry, and even more hard-hearted. Or we could press into the Lord and invite Him to use the seasons of waiting or discomfort to cultivate the soil of our hearts, trusting Him as our good, good Father.

He Is Attentive in the Waiting

My friends, can I share with you a beautiful truth? Seasons of discomfort, change, and even pain will make their way into our lives (don't worry, this isn't the beautiful truth). But when we find ourselves in these seasons, and we make a choice to press in to the Lord, we will never have to weather them alone. That is the beautiful truth! Truly, we never have to go it alone. Even in the seasons when we feel the most disconnected, lonely, or isolated in the natural world, our Father is right by our sides, putting His comforting arm around our shoulders. And when we make the intentional choice to invite the Lord into our most challenging and most cultivating seasons, we enter into a partnership with the Father. In John 15:1, Jesus tells us that His Father is the Gardener who is attentive year-round to His vineyard. Just as a farmer watches the fields to know if they need water, shade, cultivation, or nourishment to stay healthy, our Father watches His vineyard (us!) to ensure that we are healthy and have precisely what we need.

Can I share with you something else? Vines grown from the seed can take anywhere from two to seven years to produce a grape, depending on the variety! That's a long wait for a grape. Sometimes our wait is long. And when it's the seven-year-grape kind of wait instead of the two-year kind, it can be easy for doubts to settle in or fears that we've been forgotten or abandoned to spring up. But however long the wait, it's exactly the length that's needed to produce quality, healthy fruit.

Jesus understands our humanity. And I believe this is why He paints a picture we can relate to, helping us see and better understand the Father's heart. The cultivation needed for the soil can be painful, the growth process can be long, much of it occurs under the surface, and it's easy for weeds of discouragement to take root in our hearts. But our Father is the Gardener. He is always attentive, He knows exactly what we need each step of the journey, and as we continue to invite Him in and partner with Him, He will help us grow and produce fruit for His glory.

Acting in the Waiting

While the Lord is doing a lot of the heavy lifting in these seasons, we must never think we are merely along for the ride. Remember, this is a partnership. In these seasons of cultivation, the Lord is still calling us to act. He is working on our hearts, churning the dry soil, and breathing new life, and in the cultivation, He is calling us to stay faithful to the things that He has given us to do.

I understand how easy it is to feel that being faithful to cultivate the fields we are in now—over and over again—leaves us weary, seemingly without traction, or learning painfully little (at least, it feels that way sometimes). But we can rest assured that the Lord is working behind the scenes or in more profound ways not yet visible on the surface. We may see little to no movement from our finite perspective, but the Lord is working fervently in our wait until the time is right for us to see and take the next steps. John Piper once said, "God is always doing 10,000 things in your life, and you may be aware of three of them" (*Desiring God*). How humbling.

So often, I complain about my wait, wishing for a time that seems better or more fitting for me. I long for things to be different than they are. I run through scenario after scenario in my mind, and I struggle to understand why it's not a good idea to have these things now. But I only see the three. I only see *my* side of things. My part of the equation may seem small or like I'm doing painfully little, but all the while, the Lord is working out His perfect timing on *His* side of things. I can almost see Him smile as He tells me to wait just a little while longer—the fruit of this season will all be worth it.

Be Brave and Take Courage

However, even the knowledge that the Lord is cultivating us in our waits doesn't seem to keep us from worrying or falling prey to frustration and weariness. Who knew this better than David? He was anointed king at the age of 16, but he did not assume his throne until he was 30. He knew the Lord was working behind the scenes, but tending his flock, running for his life, and constantly being betrayed by those around him surely grew tiring. David knew that seasons of waiting on the Lord could be more difficult than any other season we would walk through. He knew that we would grow weary of the monotony or the struggle, the churning or the stretching. He knew that we would need to be reminded to be brave and courageous.

The Hebrew word for "wait" in Psalm 27:14 is *qavah*, which means to wait, look for, hope, or expect. In the seasons where we cannot see the sun through the clouds, and our hearts feel like they are breaking under the pressure, it takes great courage to hope. We must be brave to walk full of expectation that the Lord will move and that it will be for His good for our lives. If I could say anything at all to breathe life into a dry season or encourage you, I would say to be brave enough to still hope that the Lord has plans for you to prosper you and not to harm you, and have the courage to wait on the Lord as He works ceaselessly behind the scenes for your good.

Waiting with a Purpose

I understand as well as most what it feels like to be stuck in a season of waiting—a season of waiting characterized by change, loss, and grief. I know the aching desire for answers, or at the very least, for something to change or move forward. I know the most difficult mental shift is often to believe you are not stuck in a stagnant season; instead, you are inviting the Lord in to move while you remain faithful with the tasks He has given you as He prepares for what is coming next. And I know how difficult it is to hope for the good that we cannot yet see and expect the Lord will bring it to pass in our lives. But I also know the Lord is faithful, ever-present, and working on my behalf, even when I cannot feel or see Him.

As I write this, I believe I am in a season of cultivation. The soil of my heart is being churned and prepared, and I must return to those two choices. I could respond in anger, bitterness, and resentment; I could allow this breaking to break me. Or I could choose to press in and rest in the Father. I fully believe that the Lord can and does use these seasons of waiting and cultivation for our good, and I believe that He can do so much more in our hearts when we press into Him in these seasons. David knew waiting required courage and was well acquainted with the concept, yet just one verse before he entreated us to be brave in our waiting, he said, "I am confident I will see the Lord's goodness while I am here in the land of the living" (Psalm 27:13). The waiting didn't break him.

Waiting is not always easy, and often we do not see the reasons for our waits until we are looking back on them. But the wait is always in the Lord's hands—invite Him into that wait. Rest in the care of the Gardener, who is always attentive to His fruit. Ask the Lord to change your heart toward your circumstances and be faithful with the things He has given you to do now.

I know I must wait and that my wait is in His hands. Now, my prayer is that the Lord gives me the grace and strength—the courage and the bravery—to wait well in this season of cultivation and preparation. I cannot get caught up in the complexity of trying to figure out what's next because, for now, it's not for me to know. Right now, I must rest in the simplicity of waiting where the Lord has planted me with the hope and expectation that He is working in that wait.

I am filled with a sense of excitement and purpose now as I look at this season of *preparation*. I am filled with hope as I wonder *what the Lord is preparing me for*. My prayer lately has become simple: that I would learn and learn well what the Lord is teaching and cultivating in my heart. I'm learning that we grow more and grow deeply when we choose to partner with what the Lord is doing in our hearts.

I am willing to wait because I want to be prepared for what the Lord has in store for me. I want to be one of the hearts with good soil to receive the seed. I want to be one who yields a crop a hundred times over. I know getting there requires the cultivation of the soil of my heart. I also understand that the process to get there can often be slow, painful, and laborious. It's certainly not easy. But my prayer remains simple, despite the circumstances: "Lord, You see the future. As I choose to invite You in and rest in You during this season of preparation, would You work in my heart? And if that work means waiting, let me learn and learn well what You are growing and cultivating in my heart. I trust You as my good, good Father who always has my best interest in mind." Simple, but far from easy.

In what areas of my life is the Lord calling me to be faithful as I wait upon Him?

_____

_____

_____

_____

Heavenly Father, thank You for the promise that You are always working, even when I can't see the results of that work yet. Would You help me to stay faithful to (fill in the blank) as I wait? And by the power of Your Holy Spirit, would You help me to be brave and courageous in my wait so I can be fully prepared for whatever You have in my future? Amen.

Right now, I must rest in the simplicity of waiting where the Lord has planted me with the hope and expectation that He is working in that wait.

chapter 7

Simply Be Real…

One thing that I deeply appreciate about King David is his complete and total honesty. You never have to guess what he is thinking because he just says it. As he waits upon the Lord, you never feel like he is being fake and gliding over the messiness and disappointments of life, yet you also never feel like he is a chronic complainer. David is authentic. I love that word: *authentic*. It means that something is not false or an imitation; it is true to one's own personality, spirit, or character; it is genuine. I find it so incredibly refreshing when people can be real—natural and authentic. Truthfully, I have a hard time holding a conversation with someone who can't be real. Someone whose answer to the "How are things, really?" question is *always*, "Everything is wonderful!"

Before I go any further, let me be perfectly clear: I fully and completely believe in the comfort of the Holy Spirit, the joy of the Lord in all circumstances, and His peace that surpasses all understanding. I know (because trust me, I've been there) that it is possible to feel His peace and joy in the middle of total pain, chaos, and even grief. That's not what I'm talking about here. I'm talking about people who cannot be *real*. I truly don't think it's possible to *feel* blessed one hundred percent of the time—feelings are fickle. And I genuinely don't believe that the Lord created us that way.

As we choose to invite the Lord into each situation—the highest of highs or the lowest of lows—we feel a deep sense of peace in our spirits, but the chaos of the world still swirls around us. We are rich in spirit, but we can still feel the lack of blessing in the natural world. If we always felt blessed, where would the gap be that shows us our desperate need for Christ?

For me, it is in the seasons of grief, brokenness, and pain that I see even more clearly my need for Christ. In my humanness, I feel the despair that screams so loudly my need for Christ. When I feel the grief and the brokenness, I recognize my own limitations and call on the Lord for His perfect strength. When I abide in the Father, His peace comes as a beautifully stark contrast to the pandemonium of this world.

Just Be Real

I sincerely appreciate it when someone can be real and authentic with me. They feel a little more relatable—more human—when I hear them say that life's been a little stretching lately. You know why? Because it has been for me, too. But what I love even more than that pure honesty is when someone ends their story with, "but God …." I'm not an advocate for negativity or complaining, but I am an advocate for authenticity that points to a need for the Father.

When both my sister and cousin passed away, and my family went through an intense season of grief and change, it would have been painfully dishonest for me to tell people when they asked how I was doing that I was feeling blessed. No, I wasn't. And people knew it. I had to be honest with people—I told them it was hard. I told them I was struggling with grief. I told them I sometimes just needed to watch something lighthearted and mindless to keep my mind off the pain. But I also told them the Lord gave me strength and comfort when there weren't always people around who could. I was able to tell them that the Lord was sustaining me. And even later, I hope to tell people how the Lord birthed so much hope and restoration in that season. I hope to tell them of the lessons the Lord continues to teach me. I hope to tell them of the faithfulness of the Lord in that season. There is much the Lord is still doing in my life and the lives of my family members, and I hope to be able to tell of it. But anytime I hope to share the beauty that came, I have to share the ashes of grief. I have to be real; I have to be *authentic*.

David is a fantastic example of living an authentic life that points to the need for Christ. Time and time again, in his writings, we see him cry out in desperation. He doesn't hide his feelings, his doubts, and his pain. In Psalm 62, David writes of the grief he feels. He writes of the people who are coming against him, scheming and delighting in it all the while. Yet immediately after he writes this, he declares in verses 5 and 6, "Let all that I am wait quietly before God, for my hope is in him. He alone is my rock and my salvation, my fortress where I will not be shaken."

David is authentic and ends with a "but God ...." Why? Because he's known God's faithfulness *deeply* throughout his life. From bears and lions to giants and kings, the Lord came through for him. As David remembers these specific moments of faithfulness, he can be authentic about his struggles while still placing pure hope in the trustworthiness of his Father.

I think this is partly why so many Christ-followers find so much comfort in the Psalms—because we feel like we can relate to David. Each of us has our own struggles, feels our own grief, and at times, are so weary we wonder if we will be able to lift our heads again. Sometimes those seasons are messy, but David reminds us that we can still find rest in our faithful God when we feel this way. God is our rock and our fortress, and in Him, we will never be shaken.

He Is God of Our Reality

Reality. Does that ever sound like an uninviting word to you? It does to me, sometimes. Reality doesn't include my hopes and dreams; it doesn't incorporate what God is preparing me *for*; it just consists of the here and now. Sometimes the here and now is boring. Sometimes the here and now is painful. It's unfinished. Sometimes it's much more exciting to think about where we're headed than it is to just dwell on where we're planted.

But reality isn't merely the present. Reality also includes everything that lead up to where you are now. The pain and the struggles, the monotony and the boredom, and the beauty and the faithfulness. One of the most significant pieces of our here and now is the knowledge of everything God has brought us through. Because when we reflect on the Lord's faithfulness in our past realities, we are reminded that He is working in our present realities—no matter how painful, dull, or beautiful they may be. When we invite Him into reality, He will use it for His glory.

As I write this, reality for me is a little overwhelming. I feel overwhelmed by the decisions I'm facing, the situations I find myself in, and the vast unknowns of the future. I could allow these feelings to cripple me, rendering me useless and making it a little more difficult for the Lord to work in my life. And to be *authentic*, there are a few times when I have allowed it to cripple me in the last few months. I've given into fear, anger, and frustration. But when I take time to reflect on my past realities—the moments the Lord has faithfully directed, comforted, and encouraged—I am reminded the Lord is working even now.

My friends, there were seasons in my life when I could

not see what the Lord was doing for the life of me. But as I look back on them now, I see His loving hand directing my steps. Once, I took time to journal and reflect back on a four-year period of my life. Over several pages, I recounted every twist, turn, heartache, and victory. It was amazing to trace the path all the way to where I was at that day, preparing to head off to the next thing to which the Lord had called me. On every moment I recorded in my journal, I could see the Lord's fingerprints; I could see how He used each one to prepare me for the next thing He had in store. If you've never done something like that before, I encourage you to take the time to do so. For me, it was one of the most faith-building experiences. I could see how each moment—the painful, the boring, the confusing, the encouraging—played a *specific* and *significant* role in my life and my relationship with the Lord.

The Lord is always working. When we are authentic with the Lord and invite Him into our realities, He takes them and makes them something beautiful. Reflecting on this truth brings hope into the darkest moments. Because the truth is, sometimes our realities are messy, painful, or shameful. But He is still working. When we invite Him in, we ask Him to take the reins and do what He does best: bring beauty from the ashes.

The Lord Works Messes into Masterpieces

A few weeks ago, in prayer, the Lord gave me a mental picture that I wrote down in my journal. It helped to bring a visual to the work God does when we invite Him into our real, struggle-ridden, grief-filled, and worn lives. I was seeking the Lord, inviting Him into my life, which lately—in an effort to be authentic, here—has felt more like a mess. Almost instantly, when I pictured my life as a little messy, the Lord brought Isaiah 64:8 to mind: "And yet, O Lord, you are our Father. We are the clay, and you are the potter; we are all the work of your hand."

With that picture in my mind, this is what I wrote in my journal:

My "mess" is like freshly made clay. It is messy, made from dirt—slimy, gritty, and dripping. It's making me feel messy, and it gets on everything I touch. Why would I want to hold onto that kind of mess? If I choose to hold onto it, it will dry up and crust over and become a hard lump that weighs me down and throws me off balance. It is not only useless and ugly, but it is also a hindrance and a burden.

What if instead, I choose to hand this messy, slimy, gritty clay over to the expert Potter—the world-renowned, original Potter who created the idea of pottery and has never made a piece that is not breathtakingly beautiful? If I hand it over to Him, then He can begin to mold it and shape it. He does not cringe at the mess. He is not upset by the grit or turned off by the slime. In fact, He welcomes it—He has asked many, many times to be given it, for He knows those are all vital pieces to the finished work.

I watch as the Potter takes the mess I have given Him and begins to shape it and smooth down the rough edges. The work is a little slow, and many times, He even asks me to participate in the process of shaping and molding. I watch the shape take form, but it still looks a little flimsy. But He is not finished yet—He takes the unstable form and puts it through the fire. I feel the heat of it and wait somewhat impatiently as the fire finalizes the form. What comes out is no longer gritty, slimy, dripping, ugly, flimsy ... what comes out is a beautiful, ornate, expertly-crafted vase that is smooth and shiny. It has a purpose, and I cannot wait to use it—to put it on display for all to see what the Potter has made.

I understand now why He welcomed my mess. The mess is now beautiful, useful, and can even be given as a gift. It started out messy—it had to—and the Potter alone knew the outcome. This is why He asked time and time again for me to give Him the mess. He

welcomed it and didn't mind it because He already saw the end result:
unmatched beauty.

Each page of my journal has a different verse at the end of
it—it just so happened that the verse at the end of this page
was Ecclesiastes 3:11: "God has made everything beautiful
in its time" (NIV).

Juggling grief, moving, job transitions, disappointments,
and adulting over the past few years leaves my story looking less than picturesque. My life feels a little messy. I wonder what on earth the Lord could be up to, what He's got
planned, and how He will use the mess. All I can see right
now is the slimy, dirty lump—not the promised beauty that
will come after the shaping and the fire. Don't we all find
ourselves in places like this? Sometimes the mess looks
enormous, it overwhelms us, and we can't seem to dig our
own way out of it (friendly reminder: we weren't meant to).
Other times, the mess is an annoyance—like a few dishes in
the sink when company walks in the door.

I think the mess most often shows up when we can't
see a purpose, or it wasn't in the plan. We're left wondering:
can God make something out of this mess? I think we're in
good company ....

Abraham lied to protect himself on more than one oc-
casion, tried to rush God's plans, and allowed himself to be
influenced by others; Abraham surrendered his mess to the
Lord and became the father of many nations.

Ruth was widowed, moved countries, and had to find a
way to support herself and her elderly mother-in-law; Ruth
surrendered her mess to the Lord and married the man of
her dreams and became the great-grandmother of the king
of Israel.

David ran for his life and hid in caves, committed adultery, and had a man murdered; David surrendered his mess to the Lord and became one of Israel's greatest kings.

Remember the other thing the three of them have in common? They're in the lineage of Jesus.

We Are Molded and Shaped in His Hands

The Lord is in the business of making things beautiful in their time, and this is the gift of authenticity: He knows our messes, and He welcomes them because He sees the future of our surrendered messes when all we can see is dirt. The Lord is not asking me to take control of my mess or dig my own way out. He is calling me simply to surrender the mess to His strong, capable, and skilled hands and invite Him in to make it beautiful.

In Psalm 37:4, the Lord says to delight myself in Him, and He will give me the desires of my heart. Interestingly enough, the original Hebrew word for "delight" here is *anog*, which is literally translated as being soft or dainty. The NAS Exhaustive Concordance also adds "pliable" to the definition. When we reread the verse with this definition in mind, it now says, "Be soft, dainty, or pliable in Him ...."

When we authentically humble ourselves before the Lord and invite Him to have a hand in our messes, He molds them to match the desires of *His* heart. When we allow our hearts and lives—our mess—to be developed and shaped by the expert Potter, the desires of His heart become our own. This takes the focus off ourselves and our efforts to shape the mess and puts it back on the Lord and His work that He is making beautiful. The pressure is off our shoulders to mold the final outcome when we invite Him in to do His work. Sometimes He asks us to participate in the process, but His craftsmanship is still taking the reins.

When I choose to simply surrender the mess to the Lord and invite Him in instead of striving to fix it myself, I am freely giving Him the weight I bear and inviting Him to mold and shape something beautiful that only He can envision. When I read the stories of people in the Bible like Abraham, Ruth, or David, I am filled with so much excitement, anticipation, and hope. What is on the other side of my surrendered mess?

The Gift of Authenticity

I think David's testimony of God's faithfulness in difficulty can be our own, as well. Surrender the mess over to the Lord so He can mold and shape you into something beautiful. Ask the Father to help you see your challenges as an opportunity to encourage those around you who may also be going through difficult situations. We can even learn to see the lessons in those seasons as an honor—what a gift that the Lord would have us use the lessons we learned through difficulties to encourage someone else who may be struggling in similar seasons.

I think it's also important to note that we should not only be authentic with those around us, but we should also be authentic with the Lord. Again, I think there is no better example of this than David. He was honest with the Lord when he struggled, felt fear, and was overwhelmed. He invited the Lord into those feelings and circumstances and asked the Lord to move. By opening up about his inadequacies in those moments, he acknowledged his humanness and invited the Lord to fill that gap by molding and shaping him into something that was pleasing in the Lord's sight. Our inadequacies allow us to recognize that gaps that can only be filled by the Lord.

We will face difficulties in this life—Jesus said so in John 16:33. And I think we have a few lessons to learn from David's life when we encounter those difficulties. We need to be real about those difficulties with the Lord, surrender the mess, and invite Him to fill the gap with His perfect abundance. He is the Expert Craftsman and the Divine Potter. He has a vision for our lives that He can bring about if we allow Him to mold and shape us. When we are overwhelmed and crumbling under the weight of our mess, our invitation to Him declares that we believe He is enough. Remember the times He was enough in our past?

Side note: I think many of us suffer from short-term memory loss when it comes to the faithfulness of the Lord. I don't believe this is malicious or intentional, but I am aware of the strength of our feelings when we're deep in the midst of an overwhelming, painful, or intimidating situation. Worry and fear take over, causing us to wonder how we will get out or if the Lord will come through for us. These questions often rise above our memories of the Lord's faithfulness in the past. Will He come through *again*? Will He be faithful *this time*? How will I make it through what is going on *right now*?

In these question-filled moments, Matthew 7:9–11 reminds us of the kind of God we serve: "You parents— if your children ask for a loaf of bread, do you give them a stone instead? Or if they ask for a fish, do you give them a snake? Of course not! So if you sinful people know how to give good gifts to your children, how much more will your heavenly Father give good gifts to those who ask him."

Friends, when you're struggling to remember the Lord's faithfulness, or you're striving to rise above the weight of what's going on around you, let the truth of this Scripture wash over you. Take a step back from the striving, settle into a cozy chair, and tell the Father your struggles. Let me tell you, striving gets us nowhere. Be real. Be authentic. And come back to this verse time and time again. If those who love you in this world know how to give you good gifts, take care of you, and comfort you, how much more does your perfect heavenly Father?

The first and most simple step toward making our mess beautiful is handing it over to the Father and inviting Him in to do His work. But next, I believe we need to be authentic with those around us. We have the opportunity to share about the times when we felt inadequate, and the Lord stepped in and became enough. We have the opportunity to encourage those around us with the truth that the Lord will be faithful to meet us where we are at—struggles and all— and shape us. It goes back to the simple truth of inviting Him in … this simply goes a step further and shares that truth with others. When we are simply authentic with people, we allow our lives to become a testimony of God's faithfulness amidst the difficulty. Our lives become a testimony of God standing in the gap of our inadequacies and bringing beauty from the mess. Our lives become a testimony that God is *simply enough.*

In what areas of my life have I been striving to be perfect (or even just okay) in front of the Lord or others?

_____

_____

_____

_____

Heavenly Father, thank You for asking for my mess so that You can make it beautiful. Help me to be authentic with my mess. And help me to surrender (fill in the blank) to You today. Mold and shape my heart into a vessel to be used for Your glory. Amen.

When we authentically humble ourselves before the Lord and invite Him to have a hand in our messes, He molds them to match the desires of His heart.

chapter 8

Simply in His Care...

Sometimes it's the smallest words that carry the most meaning. Have you ever thought about that? Bigger words can certainly be more complex or uncommon. Ubiquitous, voracious, loquacious, and anything else that ends in "ous." Hold on while I grab my dictionary .... Yet while the smaller words may be easier to grasp or define, I've found they are often the weightier of the two. Love. Faith. Hope. Grace. Trust. Loquacious just means you talk a lot. But trust? Now that can't be defined in four words. It's such a small word—a word that's easy to grasp but takes some unpacking to fully understand and live out.

Trust in the Storms

The other day, I found myself pondering the meaning of this little word in a new way. It was pouring rain early in the morning; I was sitting in my chair under the soft light of my lamp, wrapped in a fuzzy blanket, with a cup of coffee in hand doing some reading. The environment was peaceful and perfectly serene. I had my curtains open, and from where I was sitting, I could see the dark gray skies and the sheets of rain coming down. Usually, when it's dark and rainy out, I feel a little gloomy, but on this particular morning, I somehow felt cozier. It was like I could see the stark contrast of the environments—the dark, cold rain outside versus the warm light and comfort of my little corner in my room. I felt tucked-in, safe, and peaceful as I watched and listened to the rain coming down outside. As I was sitting and enjoying this cozy, quiet moment, I felt the Lord impress on my heart that this is what it's like when I dwell in a trust-filled relationship with Him, abiding in His care.

Side note: I love it when real-life circumstances point to the heart of the Father. Being the black and white thinker that I am, my brain craves examples, applications, and concrete thoughts. The Lord often stretches me by teaching me abstract truths which cannot be reasoned and simply require faith to believe, but every once in a while, He reveals truth to me through very practical and concrete ways—like sitting in my chair and watching the rain outside. I feel as though moments like this are special gifts from the Lord because He knows how my brain works.

Sometimes life feels like a perfect storm. The skies darken, hiding the sun; the rain begins to pour, leaving everything with that wet dog smell; the lightning crashes and the thunder rumbles, shaking you to the core; and the wind blows, uprooting the pillars of stability to which you cling so tightly. When you are out in the middle of all of this, of course fear and anxiety set in! You worry for your safety and those around you, you hang your head low in attempts to shield yourself from the stinging pellets of rain, and you sit unprotected as the storm continues to beat you down. And simplicity? Well, that is seemingly impossible to see through the storm. As I write this, my life over the past few years feels a bit like the perfect storm, and after a while of trying to stand against the winds and rain, I just feel weary and beaten down.

He Covers Us

As I was sitting in my chair that morning, thinking over the storm of the past few months, the Lord brought Psalm 91:4 to mind:

> "He will cover you with His feathers, and under His wings you will find refuge; His faithfulness will be your shield and rampart" (NIV).

Sitting there, watching the rainfall from the safety and comfort of my chair, I understood this verse in a way I had not before. We will experience storms in life. Psalm 46:2 literally says, "*when* earthquakes come and the mountains crumble into the sea ...."

But in these storms, we can rest under His wings. It's like sitting in the comfort of your home, knowing you are safe, and watching the storm rage outside. Jesus told His disciples in John 16:33,

> "... in me you may have peace. In this world you will have trouble. But take heart! I have overcome the world" (NIV).

In this world, we will have trouble. It's a fact, and it's not always a comforting one. Yet while the world around us may be the perfect storm, Jesus says He has overcome the world. He is the one in whom we abide, He is the one who covers us, and He is the one who gives us the grace to move forward. Those facts are a lot more comforting. And they're promises we get to claim when we face trouble in this world. Abiding in the peace of His presence requires the simple step of inviting Him into a moment and claiming His promises for that moment. Not for a year from now. Not for tomorrow. For this moment, right now.

Choosing peace over fear in the storms is not an easy choice—fear is a natural, human response. Choosing peace requires a continual renewing of your mind, taking captive your thoughts, and claiming God's promises. He has promised that He will be our shield to cover and protect us while the storms rage. Claim that promise even when you feel fear creeping in. Claim that promise when you feel weary. Claim that promise when you *still* cannot see the sun through the clouds. More than a circumstances-shift, claiming this promise will bring about a heart-shift. And continue to claim it, even if you may not feel the peace immediately. Faith is standing on the promises of God, even when your feelings and life's circumstances contradict them. Stay fixed on Him! Stay fixed on His promises. Isaiah 26:3 reminds us that as we stay fixed on Him, He will keep us in a place of peace: "You will keep in perfect peace all who trust in you, all whose thoughts are fixed on you!"

He Is with Us Through the Storms

Recently, I was re-reading Psalm 121. It has to be one of my favorite Psalms by far—your heart can't help but feel hope and comfort as you read through the lines of these verses. This psalm is one of the Songs of Ascents the Israelites would sing as they journeyed to the Temple in Jerusalem for festivals. As they took each step toward the city, they would sing out the verses: "My help comes from the Lord," "The Lord keeps [us] from all harm and watches over [our] lives," and "The Lord keeps watch over [us] as [we] come and go, both now and forever." Beautiful.

But if we're honest with ourselves, I think we'd say it's a little difficult to sing out these praises when the storm is blinding and fierce. Our hearts may begin to lift with hope, and then the little doubts start to sneak in:

I might be declaring these truths, but I'm really feeling the heat right now ....
It doesn't really feel like He's watching ....
Lord, I know Your Word says You are my help, and You never sleep, but this storm is getting intense, and it feels like You could have stepped in a while ago ....

Sound familiar? As I've walked through some storms, I've learned that our circumstances will always be one of the biggest hurdles of our faith. Because if the enemy of our soul can keep us focused on the storms around us, he can keep our focus off of our good, loving, capable Father who is always watching and working tirelessly behind the scenes for us. When we look at the circumstances surrounding us and what we see is absolutely glaring back, it can be so difficult to stay focused on the unseen truths and recognize the Lord's hand is still at work. Especially when our feelings tell us otherwise.

I heard once about a woman who decided to visit a silversmith after reading Malachi 3:3: "He will sit as a refiner and purifier of silver" (NIV). As she watched the silversmith work, she casually asked if he always sat by the silver while it was over the fire or if he ever got up and did something else. The silversmith replied, "Oh! I would never leave the silver while it's in the fire! I watch the heat constantly to make sure it doesn't get too intense and damage the silver. And as the heat causes the impurities to rise to the surface, I scrape them off until I can see the reflection of my face in the silver. Then I know it is pure." Now, doesn't this sound like the God from Psalm 121? Our help comes from Him; He will not let us stumble; He never sleeps; He watches over us; He stands beside us; He keeps us from harm. This doesn't mean life will be all daisies and chocolate (although sometimes that sounds like a nice idea); instead, it means He is watching every moment of every day. My friends, we can rest knowing that He knows just what we need to be refined into pure silver—silver that reflects His face. He knows what we need, and He'll walk every step with us to that place. We are in His care. That's a promise we can cling to as we weather life's storms.

Claiming the Promises

So often, I'm afraid we do not make use of the promises in Scripture. We read over them but do not claim them for ourselves. The promises in Psalm 91:4 are ones to which we should always cling—especially when the storms of life rage. We can trust that He *will cover* us; under His wings, *we will find refuge*; and His faithfulness *will be our shield and rampart*. The Strong's Concordance breaks down these passages a bit. "He will cover" comes from the Hebrew word *cakak*, which means to hedge, overshadow, cover, or stop the approach of something. To find "refuge" in Him comes from the word *chasah*, which means to flee to for protection or to put our trust in (God). And His "faithfulness"—His *reliability, stability, and sureness*—is *tsinnah*, a large shield. This passage of Scripture tells us that He will build a hedge around us, overshadow us, cover us, and stop the approach of anything coming against us. We can flee to Him for protection and confidently place our trust in Him. He is a large shield over us that is reliable, stable, and sure. I once heard it said that faith is the Word of God painting a new picture on your heart rather than what your senses currently perceive. He is a hedge, a strong tower, a large shield—what a fantastic picture to paint in our hearts. And what an amazing promise we have the gift of claiming!

This passage in no way says the storms will magically disappear, but it does say that when the storms come, we can trust we have a safe and cozy place in which we can take refuge. In the moments of life when the storm is raging all around us, we can abide—remain, rest, dwell—in the shadow of the Almighty (Psalm 91:1). There is a deep, unshakeable level of peace that comes from trusting that you are covered, safe, shielded, and protected.

He Takes the Hits

Now, let's take Psalm 91:4 a level deeper. The verse says,

> "He will cover you with His feathers, and under His wings you will find refuge; His faithfulness will be your shield and rampart" (NIV).

During a recent time of worship at my church, we sang a song with the line, "You hold my heart." As I was worshipping, the Lord gave me the picture of a set of hands holding onto a heart. Instantly, Psalm 91:4 came to mind. In this verse, there are certainly implications for us, the readers. He will cover *us* with His feathers, and under His wings *we will find refuge*. But as we are reading this verse and claiming these promises, I think we can easily miss that there are also implications for the Lord. *He covers us*, we hide under *His wings*, and *His faithfulness will shield* us. When the storm is raging, and we rush for the safety and comfort of the great indoors, the storm doesn't go away or cease to exist. Something else is taking the brunt of the storm to keep us safe and protected. In that moment of worship, I felt the Lord saying that He is holding my heart. It's not a passive action but an active, intentional decision to shield my heart, keep it close to Him, and take the beating on Himself. I saw the Hands that held my heart, and they had holes in them; they were bleeding, ripped, and bruised.

Forgive me if I preach for a minute here, but I think we need to be reminded that not only did Christ take the beating for us on the cross to save us from the punishment of our sins, but He continues to take that beating for us to be our Comforter, our Prince of Peace, and our Healer. Isaiah 53:4–5 says,

> Surely He took up our pain and bore our suffering, yet we considered Him punished by God, stricken by Him, and afflicted. But He was pierced for our transgressions, He was crushed for our iniquities; the punishment that brought us peace was on Him, and by His wounds we are healed. (NIV)

Each of these triumphs and blessings accessible to the follower of Christ is possible only because of His suffering. His hands bear the scars of the beating He took in our stead. And the impact of what Christ did on the cross was not limited to the moment of salvation; it continues on as we walk out our Christian lives. Every day, He continues to hold our hearts in His hands. We have the promises of peace, comfort, and healing because of the beating and bruising He bore to shield us. He holds our hearts in His hands.

If the promises of Psalm 91:4 only involved us, then we know we could trust Him. He promised we could seek refuge under His wings, and He will be faithful to that promise. But how much more can we trust knowing that these promises are true because He has skin in the game? As we rest in Him, He is bearing the weight of the storms. Oh, how much confidence and trust we can have in our faithful and sacrificial God!

Scripture is filled with pictures God wants to paint in our hearts. Images that display who He is and how He cares. In Genesis 16:13, He is painted as *El Roi*—the God who sees—with Hagar in the wilderness. In Psalm 23, He is our good, good Shepherd—*Jehovah Ra'ah*. In 1 Kings 17:1–7, He is the practical Provider and uses ravens to feed Elijah. Who is He to you? As you look back over your life and your experiences with the Father, what pictures do you see Him painting? And please hear me: learn to separate your physical experiences from who God was through them. I can look back on my life and see lonely seasons, disappointing seasons, or seasons filled with grief and pain. Does this mean God abandoned me? Let me down? Unleashed His wrath on me? No. How we feel due to our circumstances is not the indicator of God's thoughts toward us. In the lonely seasons, He never left my side. In the disappointing seasons, He was my faithful God. In the seasons of grief and pain, He comforted me, held me close, and gave me hope.

My friends, we are simply taken care of. When we make the decision to invite the Lord into a moment, pause and abide in Him, and rest in His care despite what circumstances may look like, our souls are refreshed in the simplest and most profound way. We are cared for. We are covered. We can rest. In a season when all of life may feel out of control, our Father is holding us in His very hands, purifying us, and drawing us ever closer to His heart. Our job? Simply to rest in His care. Don't try to take up arms and fix a situation; instead, abide in His care and follow where His peace will lead. I've found that when we act out of a place of resting, abiding, and care, our actions are faith-based instead of fear-based. We operate out of the confidence that we are simply and definitively cared for by our heavenly Father.

As I look back over difficult seasons or situations in my past, who was God to me?

_____

_____

_____

_____

Heavenly Father, thank You. Thank You for being my good, good Father who has never left my side. Forgive me for projecting the hurt of life's circumstances onto Your character. Help me to rest in You and remember Your faithfulness. Amen.

Faith is standing on the promises of God, even when your feelings and life's circumstances contradict them.

chapter 9

Simply Trusting...

_____

I placed this chapter directly after "Simply in His Care..." on purpose. When we understand that we are in the Lord's care, that He has made specific promises to care for us, and that He has skin in the game, we can more fully and completely trust in Him. Trust. What a small word, yet literally packed with meaning and significance. In the simplest terms, the word means having a *firm* belief in the reliability, truth, ability, or strength of someone or something. That certainly holds a lot of weight. When you trust someone or something, you firmly believe that person or thing will come through for you. The word leaves no room for questions. Trust is that moment when you leap off the edge in full commitment, believing you will be caught. It's the iconic step Indiana Jones took in *The Last Crusade*—the step of faith—believing that even though he could not see the invisible bridge, he would not plummet. That's trust.

Interestingly enough, the English word for "trust" is an abstract—something that cannot be sensed by the five senses. The several different Hebrew words for "trust," however, are concrete. *Chasah* means to flee to someone or something and know that you will be supported. *Yachal* is believing in the strength of someone to rescue or save you. *Aman* means to be firm—believing that the ground upon which you stand is firm. In the 134 instances the word "trust" appears in Scripture, time and time again, it points to our ability to *flee to the Lord, knowing that we will be supported and protected, believe in His strength to rescue and save us, and stand with confidence, knowing that the ground on which we stand (Him) is firm.* The Lord has built an incredible track record with His people. I have searched the Scriptures and have yet to find one time the Lord was found not trustworthy.

Sometimes life is challenging, to say the least. We look around us, and we see disease, heartache, missed hopes and dreams, and longings unfulfilled. As we observe what's going on around us, feelings begin to surface: disappointment, grief, fear, anger. The situation seems dismal, and we're left feeling overwhelmed and defeated. As we focus on our circumstances, it's painfully easy for our trust to wane. It's here that we reach a crossroads in our hearts: will we dwell in the truth of our troubles? Or will we dwell in the truth that our Lord is worthy of our trust? To dwell somewhere means that we remain for a time in that place, live there as a resident, or keep our attention directed on it. Will we *dwell* on our troubles as the truth we see and believe? *Or* will we invite the Lord into what we see around us and remain, live, and keep our attention on His promises as our truth?

A Trustworthy Track Record

The circumstances swirling around us are real—they have real implications, and real feelings follow them. But, my friends, even more real than our circumstances are the promises of our God. His promises have been tested and tried, and they have proven faithful. You remember from the last chapter that we are like silver being purified. But Scripture also says the Lord's promises go through that process, as well. In Psalm 12:6, the psalmist writes that the promises of the Lord "are pure, like silver refined in a furnace, purified seven times over." When silver goes through the purification process, it's heated to temperatures of up to 1,450°F. As the molten mixture bubbles and simmers, the heavier silver sinks to the bottom, and the lighter impurities (dross) rise to the surface. The silversmith painstakingly and repeatedly scrapes the waste off the top. The silver must undergo severe heat and testing, but when the silversmith finally removes the last of the dross from the surface and sees his reflection in the silver, he knows it is *pure*.

The Lord's promises are like silver purified *seven times over*. His promises haven't merely proven true and trustworthy in light seasons when we claim them as an afterthought. His promises have withstood the heat and pressure of circumstances that beg us to *cling* to them. And if we look into every one of His promises, we can see a reflection of His face—what a picture of His love and faithfulness to which we can cling. Yes, we live in a world where we will experience trouble. We can lament. We can grieve. We can long for heaven. But the Lord is our rescuer. He has a track record that has proven *trustworthy*. The promises He has made to us are tested, pure, and a reflection of His face.

I believe we were created with an intrinsic need to know we can trust or feel safe with someone or something. We are hurt and disappointed when a friend or family member lets us down. We are angry and frustrated when our car doesn't start in the morning like it's supposed to. We crave the knowledge that we have someone or something we can trust. And the better the track record, the more we believe we can trust. The more reliable the source, the more we feel at rest with it. When a friend or family member proves themselves trustworthy time and time again, we are more inclined to trust them. When your car starts reliably every single morning, we never give it a second thought that it might do otherwise. The more something comes through for us, the more we believe that it will come through again in the future.

Altars of Stones

I'm a huge advocate for prayer journals. I think it is incredibly cathartic to put your thoughts and emotions and prayers on a piece of paper, essentially permitting yourself to release them from your mind because you've immortalized them on paper. I've journaled through some of my most challenging seasons, and it helped bring clarity to the mess by simply writing out my thoughts.

But I don't believe in the importance of prayer journaling merely for the healing it can bring in the moment. In fact, I think the most important reason we journal out our prayers is so we can look back on them and examine the times the Lord Himself has come through for us. His promises have withstood the testing and the fire—they are pure. Trust: firm belief in the reliability, truth, ability, or strength of someone or something. The more you have tested the reliability, truth, ability, or strength of someone or something, the more firm your belief in that thing becomes. I will be the first to admit that I have prayed so many prayers over my lifetime that I have certainly forgotten a chunk of them after I prayed them. Rereading my conversations with the Lord brings back prayers I forgot I prayed and as a result, almost didn't realize the Lord had faithfully answered. My trust grows.

Keeping something as simple as a prayer journal is a beautiful personal reminder of that track record in our own lives. In the Old Testament, the Israelites constructed small altars of stones at the place where the Lord had been faithful to them. They did this as a permanent reminder of the Lord's faithfulness, so whenever they revisited that place, they would remember how the Lord had been faithful. Prayer journaling acts as our own altar of stones, reminding us of the faithfulness of the Lord in our own life each time we revisit it.

In Psalm 77, Asaph, David's chief musician, had a moment of reflecting on the altars of stones in the history of the nation of Israel. At the start of the chapter, he raises some painfully honest questions. Questions I think we've all found ourselves asking at one time or another: *Has the Lord rejected me? Has He forgotten to be gracious? Is His unfailing love gone forever? Have His promises failed?* I think we can all agree how easy it is to feel overwhelmed by the weight of what's going on around us. We struggle with feeling too distressed even to pray.

As we read further in the chapter, however, we come across a beautiful shift. In Psalm 77:11, Asaph uses one powerful word that dynamically alters the trajectory of his thinking: *but.* He says, "But then I recall all you have done, O Lord; I remember your wonderful deeds of long ago."

From that point on, the chapter becomes one of praise for all the Lord had done for His people. As the reader, you feel a distinct shift in the tone of the chapter. But there is something key here I believe we need to fully grasp and understand: the circumstances surrounding Asaph did not change. His circumstances were still very much the same; the difference is that he brought God's track record of faithfulness into the mix.

We live in an overwhelming world right now. All we have to do is scroll through social media or flip on the news, and we are literally bombarded with discouragement and despair. I feel it! I know you do, too. But I also know we serve a God who has been faithful in the past and who has promised He will be faithful again. Our circumstances may not shift, but I promise you there is a heart-shift when we choose to see our current circumstances in the light of His past record of faithfulness.

As we reflect on the wilderness seasons He has already brought us through, our faith begins to grow. Faith is looking at our overwhelming circumstances in the light of a faithful God. Worry and anxiety set in when we look at our overwhelming circumstances in the dimness of our own strength and understanding. We can't keep our eyes closed to what's happening around us, but my friends, let's look instead with eyes lit up by the faithfulness of our Father and who He is to us.

I think it is one of the most faith-building exercises to look back on our lives and revisit the moments of the Lord's faithfulness. We glance back on the times in our lives we hope never to relive, but amidst all of the pain, confusion, waiting, and frustration, we see the light of the Lord's fingerprints in a way we've never seen them before. I know if the Lord can get me through *that*, He can be faithful to get me through anything. Amazingly enough, even though we think that at the moment, it is still so easy to forget once the next trial rears its ugly head. This is why we must return time and time again to the altars of stones in our own lives. But while we revisit those places, we cannot fall into the trap of thinking that the Lord will resolve our current situation in the same way He did in the past.

Trust in the Lord, Not the System

I once heard a pastor preach on Isaiah 43:15–19. It's an incredible Scripture in which the Lord reminds the people of Israel of all He had done for them: He made a way through the sea, rescued them from the Egyptian army, and kept them from returning to slavery. But at the end of the passage, after He reminded them of all He had done for them, He said,

> "Forget the former things; do not dwell on the past. See, I am doing a new thing!" (Isaiah 43:18–19, NIV).

It's almost baffling that the Lord would remind His people of all He had done and then say, "Now forget those things." But in essence, the Lord was saying, "Remember *that* I did them; forget *how* I did them. I will be faithful, but not always in the same way." If the Lord were to be faithful in the same way in our lives every single time, I'm afraid we would become dependent upon a system instead of the Lord.

In Exodus 17, the Israelites were out of water, so the Lord commanded Moses to strike a rock. Later in Numbers 20, the same situation presented itself, but the Lord told Moses to speak to the rock instead of hitting it. In fear, Moses struck the rock because he fell prey to trusting a system more than he trusted the faithfulness of the Lord. Forget *how* the Lord has been faithful in your life because He will likely not do it that way again, but never forget *that* He was faithful. Look back on the Lord's track record in your life and allow it to be a time of trust-building.

Trust When You Don't Have the Details

Sometimes the simple act of inviting the Lord into the storm and trusting Him through the chaos is the most challenging task, because even though He has been faithful before, it almost seems impossible this time. We don't understand how the situation could resolve itself, we don't see the end to our wait, or something seems too unbelievable to be true. Or I find more often, things just don't make sense. We find ourselves circling our understanding of our current season with more questions than answers. *"Lord, I thought this was where You wanted me to go, but it feels like You're taking me in the opposite direction! I don't get why You have me here right now. I'm trying to understand Your will, but this doesn't make sense to me."* Sound familiar?

I love the New Living Translation of Proverbs 20:24, which says, "The Lord directs our steps, so why try to understand everything along the way?" Imagine you are driving through a new town. You are in the car with a friend who is acting as your trusted DJ and navigator. You have no clue where you are headed, but your friend does because they have the map. They don't tell you all of the turns you will need to make to get to your destination right away because that would be information overload, and you would definitely get lost along the way. They tell you when your next turn is, and you follow their instructions. Occasionally, you make a wrong turn, and they have to reset your course. Other times, they tell you to turn in a direction that feels like the opposite way from where you are supposed to be headed. You trust that friend and their map, so you don't question when they tell you to turn. In fact, you mostly do it without thinking, and once you've made your turn, you look to them for the next step. Sometimes those next turns come right away, and other times, you're on the same road for several miles. Either way, your friend knows where you're headed and will tell you the next step when you need to know it. You, as the driver, don't always understand how all of the turns come together to create the way to your destination; you just know that your friend knows the destination and exactly what it will take to get there. In essence, you get the turn-by-turn, and your friend has the overview.

I think this is precisely where we need to be as we trust and abide in the Lord. He knows our destinations and can see all of the turns it will take to get us there. Sometimes we make a wrong turn, but if we look to Him for our direction, He will correct us. (I think it's worth saying here that our course is not ruined, and our destination not rendered unreachable if we make a wrong turn. There might be some delays, but we simply have to turn to the Lord for direction, and He gives us the course-correct.) Romans 8:28 says,

> "And we know that God causes everything to work together for the good of those who love God and are called according to his purpose for them."

Everything. This does not mean life will always turn out perfectly, but it does mean God is working in the midst and bringing about His good for those who love Him and are called according to His purpose. These aren't the people who do it all perfectly. These are the people who return to Him for the course-correct.

Other times, He has us make turns that feel like we're headed in the opposite direction of where we thought the destination was. But He holds the map, and He can see the bird's-eye view; He knows how to get us to where we need to go. Our job is to surrender our need to understand everything along the way. I think we could even go as far as to say that if we took the time and energy to try and understand every turn, we would likely get so side-tracked and distracted we might not hear His instructions and miss our next turn. Instead of grappling for understanding, we simply rest in trusting that the Lord knows our destination and He is directing our steps. And it becomes relational as we listen for His voice instead of merely remembering the steps or following a system.

Trust When We Can't See the End

Trusting the Lord means leaning not on our own understanding (Proverbs 3:5) and instead, leaning on Him who will guide us, support us, be our strong defender, and the firm ground upon which we can stand. We struggle to stand and to trust now because we cannot see the resolution but take heart! David couldn't see the resolution as he gathered the stones for his slingshot, Abraham couldn't see the resolution as he walked up the mountain to sacrifice his son, and Ruth couldn't see the resolution as she painstakingly gathered grain in the fields every day. We look back on those stories thinking it would be silly not to trust the Lord because we know how those stories end: the Lord is faithful.

The giant is dead, the son became the patriarch of a great nation, and Ruth found love and protection, and all of them—imperfect as they were—are in the lineage of Christ. Scripture is full of people who could not see the resolution but trusted in a faithful God. In my own life, there are areas in which I cannot see the answer. But I have to believe that I serve a trustworthy God. I have to believe that I will look back and think myself silly for thinking even for an instant that I could not trust.

Trust, while simple, is one of the hardest things we will ever do in our lives. Trust is saying that I do not hold to my own understanding of the world and my own expectations in life. Trust is saying I believe—whether I see it or not—that the Lord is strong, He will uphold me, He will fight for me, and He is the firm rock upon which I can stand. Trust is saying I may not understand, but I will still have faith. When we make the conscious decision to trust, we are literally resting in the shadow of His wings. We are choosing to abide in Him and say, "You are the vine, and I am the branches. You are my source, and everything I am is because of You."

The core of the simplest thing in our relationship with the Lord is *trust*. If we did not trust, we would not rest. If we did not trust, we would not abide. If we did not trust, we would try to make sense of the storm and chaos on our own. If we did not trust, we would begin everything in our own strength and be forced to maintain everything by our own strength. It won't always make sense. And I'm sorry if I'm disappointing you to say that it will, in fact, very *rarely* make sense to us. But despite the muddled view, the uncertainty, and the questions, we know we can trust our God. His track record is flawless, His promises have been through the fire, and He is holding our hearts in His hands. When the world is overwhelming and seemingly splitting at the seams, we can take a step back and invite Him in. We can rest in Him. We can trust Him. Not easy at all, but incredibly simple.

As I look back over my faith journey, what do I recognize as my altars of stones?

_____

_____

_____

_____

Heavenly Father, thank You for being my firm foundation, protection, and solid rock. Thank You for reminding me of my altars of stones— the times on which I can look back and remember Your faithfulness. You have come through for me before, and I believe You will do it again. Help me in my unbelief. Amen.

Trust is saying I believe—whether I see it or not—that the Lord is strong, He will uphold me, He will fight for me, and He is the firm rock upon which I can stand.

chapter 10
Simply Be Still...

———

Sometimes it just feels nice to sit down. Have you heard that before? Chances are, you've probably said it yourself. And isn't it true? In a world where we *constantly* rush, race, plan, and do, sometimes it just feels nice to sit down. To rest.

Our society has become permeated with the desire—the *need*—to forsake simplicity and fire on all cylinders at all times. We can't stand to be still. When was the last time that you just sat for the sake of sitting? No phone in hand, no book opened, no TV playing. You simply sat and breathed? Truthfully, I am having a bit of a hard time remembering, myself.

Work Versus Busy
Before I go much deeper with my thoughts, I want to clarify the difference between work and busy, because there is one. Each of us is called to work or a job; you can find multiple examples in Scripture that back this up. When God first created Adam, it says in Genesis 2:15 that the Lord took the man and put him in the Garden to *work* it and take care of it. The very first man God created, He gave a job, setting the precedence for all men to follow.

Colossians 3:23 says, "Whatever you do, work at it with all your heart, as working for the Lord, not for human masters" (NIV).

1 Timothy 5:8 goes as far as to say, "Anyone who does not provide for their relatives, and especially for their own household, has denied the faith and is worse than an unbeliever" (NIV).

And Ecclesiastes 3:12–13 highlights the joy we experience when we work well: "I know that there is nothing better for people than to be happy and to do good while they live. That each of them may eat and drink and find satisfaction in all their toil—this is the gift of God" (NIV).

We were created to work, we should work as unto the Lord, and when we do this work well, we feel a deep sense of satisfaction because it is a gift from God.

I discussed this subject with my mom the other day, and I told her about all I had accomplished that day. It was a Saturday—I got up early, spent time with the Lord, went to the gym, did my grocery shopping, finished the laundry, and cooked and baked meals for the week. I felt incredibly productive with my time, and I was looking forward to relaxing and watching a movie. It felt like a perfectly well-rounded day. As I shared my thoughts with her, I mused that the reason it felt like such a fantastic day was because this is what we were created to do. If we look at the model the Lord left for us when He created the universe and more, He worked hard for six days, and then He rested. On an obviously smaller scale, I worked hard, felt productive, and was excited to rest. It truly is so satisfying to work hard and walk away knowing that you left a job well-done.

We were created for this work.

There is a difference between work and busy. If we even look at the dictionary definitions, we can see a pretty clear distinction between them. "Work" is defined as activity involving mental or physical effort done in order to achieve a purpose or result. "Busy" is defined as having a great deal to do; to keep occupied. If you notice, the definition of work includes finite words—words that have limits or bounds: activity … to achieve a *purpose* or *result*. There are ends to the activity. The definition of busy includes words that are a little less finite: having a *great deal* to do; to *keep occupied*. This definition makes you feel as if busy goes on for a while—you have a great deal to do, and things are actively keeping you occupied. Sound familiar?

We live in a world that has a great deal to do—people are continually filling their schedules, taking on tasks, and wishing they had more hours in the day to get everything done. And heaven forbid if we don't have something to keep us occupied. We seem to be afraid of silence, of stillness, of having nothing to do. There's even a name for it. *Sedatephobia*: the fear of silence.

Okay, so there's a difference between work and busy. I do my work well, and I keep myself busy. What's the harm in that? To revisit my opening thoughts, I think we have lost our appreciation—our *ability* to simply be still, sit, rest, and abide. And we face this struggle in both our physical lives as well as our spiritual lives.

Life Happens, but God's Got It

One of my favorite chapters in the entire Bible is Psalm 46, and it really dives into what it means to be still when the world is swirling in chaos around us. I think it's worth taking a minute to reflect on the passage:

God is our refuge and strength, an ever-present help in trouble. Therefore we will not fear, though the earth give way and the mountains fall into the heart of the sea, though its waters roar and foam and the mountains quake with their surging. There is a river whose streams make glad the city of God, the holy place where the Most High dwells. God is within her, she will not fall; God will help her at break of day. Nations are in uproar, kingdoms fall; he lifts his voice, the earth melts. The Lord Almighty is with us; the God of Jacob is our fortress. Come and see what the Lord has done, the desolations he has brought on the earth. He makes wars cease to the ends of the earth. He breaks the bow and shatters the spear; he burns the shields with fire. He says, "Be still, and know that I am God; I will be exalted among the nations, I will be exalted in the earth." The Lord Almighty is with us; the God of Jacob is our fortress. (Psalm 46, NIV)

If I could summarize this passage in one sentence, it would be: life happens, but God's got it.

Notice the way the author writes the first few verses: "*though* the earth give way and the mountains fall into the heart of the sea, *though* its waters roar and foam and the mountains quake with their surging ...." It just gives you a sense of inevitability, doesn't it? There's no comforting possibility of *if* the earth gives way or *maybe* the waters will roar. The New Living Translation even says, "*when* earthquakes come and mountains crumble into the sea."

Now translate these first few verses into real earthquakes and surging seas in our own lives: *when* a loved one passes away; *when* my company downsizes, and I lose my job; *when* I followed the call of the Lord, and it isn't turning out how I thought it would; *when* I am living paycheck to paycheck and struggling to make ends meet; *when* I am in a season of waiting and loneliness, and I can't seem to see the sun through the clouds; *when* I … fill in the blank. This passage leaves me with no room to guess that there will be earthquakes and surging seas in my life. Sometimes just getting through a day with all I have planned (or others have planned) seems like an earthquake, a tornado, and a tsunami all wrapped into one.

But the reason this passage of Scripture is a chart-topper for me is not because of the reminder of the certain trials I will face in this world (shocking, I know). It is the reminder line after line that though these troubles assail us:

> *God is our refuge and strength, an ever-present help in trouble.*
> *God is within her, she will not fall; God will help her at break of day.*
> *The Lord Almighty is with us; the God of Jacob is our fortress.*
> *He says, "Be still, and know that I am God."*
> *The Lord Almighty is with us; the God of Jacob is our fortress.*

Line after line proclaims the truth that life happens, but God's got it. And remember that Jesus echoes this sentiment in John 16:33,

> "I have told you these things, so that in me you may have peace. In this world, you will have trouble. But take heart! I have overcome the world" (NIV).

Troubles will come in this world. But this world has been overcome by Jesus Himself, who gives us the supernatural grace to forgive, heal, and surmount whatever comes our way.

Let Your Hands Drop

What beautiful and reassuring promises from the Word of

God! This truth that God will fight for us, uphold us, and be our refuge and strength is what gets me up each morning and keeps me going. But the Scripture doesn't stop there. Please listen closely: while the Lord will uphold us, stay right by our sides, and be our strong fortress, this in no way, shape, or form means that we do nothing—we have a job to do. This passage in Psalms reminds us that God's got it, but for Him to have it fully and completely, we must *let go of it*. Sometimes, this seems like one of the most challenging callings on our Christian journeys—letting go of the things we hold so tightly. The dream we've been working toward for years; the restored relationship we've prayed for ceaselessly; the stability we crave so deeply when everything seems so out of our control; the schedule we have so meticulously planned for our day; the joy we chase because life's circumstances have left us deflated.

We hold tightly to these often good and exciting things, not fully letting the realization sink in that when we hold tightly to something and try to bring it to pass on our end, we've taken it out of God's hands and into our own. We've added it to our list of to-dos, and we're trying to run with it on our own. But how can God fully and completely protect something that He is not holding?

Now, please don't misunderstand me: I believe God is fully capable of doing anything and everything, but I also believe He gave us the ability to choose. One of the choices we face daily is if we will pick things up out of His hands and try to run with them on our own. And each time we do, we pile unnecessary busyness onto our days. We add those little tasks to our mental to-do lists, and we charge ahead with the reins in our own hands. Yet, I think we make it pretty hard on God when we choose to take the reins; trust me, I know. When we worry, we pick up the reins. When we act after God says wait, we pick up the reins. Truth be told,

I pick up the reins every single day about something. I love feeling like I'm in control, and I know the outcome. This is probably why I love cleaning so much … I'm in total control, and there is instant satisfaction! Dirty surface? Wipe it with Windex and a microfiber cloth and poof! Clean. Complete control over the outcome and instant satisfaction. Oh, how I wish life were as simple as a cleaning day sometimes.

But in the busyness of life, the Lord doesn't call us to take up the Windex and microfiber cloth. He doesn't call us to rush and run, filling our schedule with our own list of to-dos. He doesn't hand us the map and tell us to be the navigator of the trip. He doesn't ask us to take control. In fact, He calls us to something much more simple. He asks us to take those to-dos off of our list and hand them to Him. In Psalm 46:10, He says, "Be still, and know that I am God."

The original Hebrew word used in this verse for "be still" was *raphah*, which literally translated means to slack or let drop. Contextually, this word was used when workers let their hands drop from their work. Interesting. *Yadah* is the Hebrew word used for "know." It is the same word used to describe intimacy in marriage. This intimacy only comes from experiencing relationship at the deepest level. This verse now reads: "Let your hands drop from your work, and experience relationship with your God at the deepest level." The Lord created us for work, but He also knows we were created with a void that we will try to fill with work and busyness when it was only meant to be filled with Him. Work is a good and beautiful thing, but when it takes precedence over a relationship with Him and *abiding* in Him in a place of peace, we find a problem. Work has transitioned over to busy, and we are so occupied that we miss Him right in our midst, waiting to be invited in.

Sit with Him

One of my favorite stories in Scripture is found in Luke 10:38–42. It reads:

> As Jesus and the disciples continued on their way to Je-
> rusalem, they came to a certain village where a woman
> named Martha welcomed him into her home. Her sister,
> Mary, sat at the Lord's feet, listening to what he taught.
> But Martha was distracted by the big dinner she was
> preparing. She came to Jesus and said, "Lord, doesn't
> it seem unfair to you that my sister just sits here while I
> do all the work? Tell her to come and help me." But the
> Lord said to her, "My dear Martha, you are worried and
> upset over all these details! There is only one thing worth
> being concerned about. Mary has discovered it, and it
> will not be taken away from her."

Before we jump to addressing Martha's errors in this story,
let's put ourselves in her shoes. Imagine that one of the most
influential teachers of the Christian movement was coming
to your home—let's pick John Bevere for now. Imagine that
John Bevere was coming to your home, and dinner was not
ready yet, there were still a few random articles of clothing
strewn about the house, and you needed to set the table. I
can imagine that you would scurry around getting all of the
details in place because you want Mr. Bevere to feel honored
and respected during his time in your home. At least, I think
that's how I would respond if he came to my house.

This was Martha's response to Jesus when He came to
her home. The Amplified Bible even says she was very *busy*
and distracted by all of her serving responsibilities. Her opportunity to serve the Lord took over her chance to spend
time with the Lord—to invest in a relationship with Him. We
are commanded to work, serve the Lord with our gifts, and

work as unto the Lord in all we do. But Jesus makes a very clear caveat to our work: it is good *until* it takes away from our relationship with Him. It is good *until* we attempt to make it fill the void that can only be filled by spending time sitting at the feet of Jesus. And an excellent barometer to know if I've crossed the line from resting in relationship to work and busyness is my lack of peace. Work is temporary; relationship with Jesus is eternal, and "it will not be taken away from [us]."

For God to fight for us and protect us in the most secure way possible, we must let our hands drop from the work and seek intimacy with Him above all else. The Father entreats us to release our grip on control, invite Him in, and embrace relationship with Him. This command is simple, but if I must confess, often far from easy. We must simply open our hands before the Lord, approach Him with a soft heart, and hand over that to which we have been clinging so tightly. And let me tell you, sometimes I make this journey with my heels dug in, feeling anything but release. It is a process of continuing to open our hands and release our control. Sometimes all we can say is, "Lord, I release my hold on (fill in the blank) to You. Please take the reins." And He will. He has promised that He will.

Never feel shame or guilt when you instinctively pick that thing back up; just share a knowing smile with the Lord and say "Oh, I did it again!" and hand it right back. If you're anything like me, you'll have to do this quite a few times ... a day. It's certainly a process. But I am so thankful the Lord didn't make it a complicated one. He made it simple, knowing I would struggle with it day after day. But the Lord also knows the more I invite Him in, abide in Him, and *know* Him, the more I will be able to trust Him because out of this deep intimacy comes trust. Are you finding it difficult to trust Him right now? Then invite Him in and *know* Him more. Search the Scriptures to find out more about Him. We can more fully release that which we've been holding onto when we fully trust the God that we *know*.

For many of us, simply sitting still is often one of the most challenging tasks we could envision for ourselves. We are so used to the hustle and bustle, we are addicted to busy, and it may even feel wasteful to sit and do nothing. But, my friends, s*itting at the feet of Jesus* is far from wasteful. Quieting our hearts and minds, putting away the distractions, and breathing deep in the presence of the Lord is a vital and *active* piece of our relationship with Him. We are actively creating a space in which He can speak to us. I imagine that Martha, in all her busyness, had trouble hearing what the Lord was saying in the next room as He taught. She likely knew that He was speaking, but she was so distracted by all she felt she needed to do, she could not hear His voice the way that Mary, who sat at the Savior's feet, could listen to and understand. The Lord said Mary chose the one thing that was better—the one thing that could truly and completely fill the void with which we were created— and that one thing would never be taken away from her.

Sitting still and putting away all distractions is arguably one of the simplest things we could ever do because it requires *doing* nothing. Unfortunately, for many of us, with the influences of the world and how our brains have been programmed, this task will be far from easy. And when you start out, your mind may be crowded with thoughts of all you need to get done. Keep a notepad nearby, write them all down, and then ask the Lord to help you quiet your heart and mind as you focus on the one thing—the most important thing—sitting at His feet. Open your hands, let your work drop, and hand it over to a God you know intimately. Not easy, but simple.

What is the Lord calling me to set down so that I may simply sit at His feet and know Him more?

_____

_____

_____

_____

Heavenly Father, thank You for being so readily available that all I need to do is pause to sit at Your feet and engage in relationship with You. Lord, You know my tendencies toward busyness and hurry. Help me to remember to pause and rest in my relationship with You. Help me to know You more deeply and more intimately today. Amen.

For God to fight for us and protect us in the most secure way possible, we must let our hands drop from the work and seek intimacy with Him above all else.

chapter 11

Simply Thankful...

—————

You know those seasons when you keep stumbling upon the same message, time after time, wherever you seem to turn? Over the last several weeks, my two devotional books and daily reading all seem to keep landing on the same message. Interestingly enough, it's not an easy message. It's a challenging and stretching message; truthfully, it's one I don't particularly desire to practice. Now, I know the Lord too well to think this mere coincidence—especially when it's challenging the way I think—so I'm starting to pay attention.

Everywhere I turn, the Lord is telling me to be *thankful*. In my research, I found that words used to describe "giving thanks" or "praise" are used approximately 385 times throughout Scripture, depending on your translation. Clearly, a thankful heart is something vitally important to the Lord. It's not surprising ... thankfulness is a necessary step in our relationship with the Lord. As we pause on thanksgiving, we reflect on His faithfulness, His love, and His desire to engage in relationship with us. We actively take a step back from our circumstances and invite the Lord to work despite what we can see around us. When we practice giving thanks, we intentionally recognize the work He longs to do in our hearts.

Thankful in It All

Sometimes thankfulness comes easily and swiftly—you pray a prayer, and you receive the answer for which you were hoping. *Thankfulness is easy.*

You are blessed unexpectedly with a bonus at your job. *Thankfulness is easy.*

You look around and find yourself surrounded by a life-giving community. *Thankfulness is easy.*

But let's be brutally honest, shall we? Sometimes, thankfulness doesn't come easily at all. What about thanking the Lord in the trials? When it's truly painful? When you can't see the light at the end of the tunnel? I'm in a season where—in the natural world—I feel as though I have little for which to be thankful. I'm still navigating grief, facing the pressures of adulting, and unexpected obstacles and challenges continue to rear their seemingly ugly heads. But let's pause for a moment of conviction (for you and me both). In every season, it could seem as though we have little to be thankful for—some more than others, certainly—but in our decaying world and our self-focused minds, we will always find hardships in our lives. There will *always* be things in our lives that we approach the Lord with, begging Him to change.

Even as the beloved of the Most High God, we were never promised ease and comfort. In fact, we were promised quite the opposite. Remember again what Jesus said in John 16:33—in this world, we *will* have trouble. He has overcome this world and equips us with everything we need to overcome as well, but we will still face trials and difficulty. In this imperfect world full of sin and destruction, we will be stretched, we will grieve, and we will feel uncomfortable. But I am learning it is our *responses* to the stretching, grieving, and discomfort that define our outcomes.

The Lord asks me to be thankful, not to ignore the

pain and struggles, but to turn my focus to Him amidst it all and invite Him to work within the struggles. I could grow resentful, angry, frustrated, and bitter, ripping my attention away from the Lord and feeding my own self-ishness. And honestly, sometimes that seems the more natural and welcoming option. I don't want to be thankful when life is complicated. But if I choose this route, I limit *significantly* the work the Lord can do in and through me. If instead, I decide to press into the Lord and thank Him through the suffering, the Lord can work His grace, peace, joy, and strength into my life. My thankfulness becomes a conduit of His work. The key to understanding thankful-ness amidst difficulty is recognizing that our thankfulness has more to do with *Who* we are thanking than *what* we are thankful for.

The Sacrifice of Thanksgiving

Recently in my reading, I came across Psalm 50, which has a great deal to say about being thankful. Verses 8 through 15 tell of the importance of a grateful heart to the Lord. In this verse, the Lord tells Asaph, one of David's chief musicians, that He does not need the sacrifice of bulls, birds, or goats, for the Lord owns all of the cattle on a thousand hills, and everything in the earth is the Lord's. Instead, the Lord says,

> "Make thankfulness your sacrifice to God, and keep the vows you made to the Most High. Then call on me when you are in trouble, and I will rescue you, and you will give me glory" (Psalm 50:14–15).

Later on, in verse 23, the Lord says, "But giving thanks is a sacrifice that truly honors me. If you keep to my path, I will reveal to you the salvation of God." There are a couple of key things from this chapter that I want to point out: first, the word *sacrifice*. When we offer up a sacrifice, we are giving up something *costly* to us. There is a reason that the Lord didn't ask for our *gift* of thanksgiving; He knew this would be costly to us.

If you've ever taken time to read through the book of Leviticus, then you know the sacrifices which were accept-able to the Lord were the costly belongings of the Israelites: the choicest flour and oil, the firstborn lamb, bulls without blemish. These sacrifices weren't afterthoughts or things the Israelites couldn't use for their daily life. It wasn't the old and moldy flour or the animals that were crippled and couldn't be put to work. It was the first and the best—the most *costly*. He knew there would be seasons we would walk through when the *sacrifice of thanksgiving* would be the most difficult we could make.

The second thing I want to point out in this verse is the amazing promises that follow a thankful heart: if we make thankfulness our sacrifice, then the Lord will rescue us in trouble, and we will bring Him glory! I want nothing more than for the Lord to rescue me in trouble and for my life to bring Him glory, and He says for this to happen, I must offer Him my sacrifice of thanksgiving.

Thankfulness Changes Me

I think the Lord knows something about thankfulness that we do not recognize as quickly: thankfulness prepares our hearts for the molding and shaping of the Lord. When I choose to say, "Lord, this is hard, but I will choose to thank You for (insert specifics). This is an opportunity for You to work in my life and for You to show Yourself faithful." It's painful—kind of like ripping off the band-aid—but it soft-ens our hearts to the work of the Lord. Thankfulness amidst difficulty acknowledges that His ways are not our ways, and His thoughts are higher than our thoughts (Isaiah 55:8).

Thankfulness is our way of telling the Lord that we already trust Him to work His will and His best in our lives, even when we cannot see it with our natural eyes. Even when we cannot see it, He's working. Even when we cannot feel it, He's working ("Waymaker").

One of my favorite quotes says, "We pray asking God to change our circumstances, not knowing that He put us in the circumstances to *change us.*" How humbling. The Lord knows me better than even I know myself, and He saw something in me that could be refined, purified, sharpened, or strengthened. He is simply asking for me to offer up my sacrifice of thanksgiving so He can continue the good work He began in my life and ultimately bring Him glory.

This quote also reminds me of the incredible goodness of the Father. We live in a sin-stained world where people make choices each and every day to live outside of the will of God. The decisions that others (and ourselves) make can put us in painful, difficult, irritating, and draining circumstances. Still, God, in His incredible goodness, can use even those circumstances to bring about something beautiful.

Thankful for Beauty from the Ashes

Recently, a dear friend lost her sister very suddenly. Days after receiving the news of her sister's passing, I was sitting with her and listening as she processed some of her thoughts and emotions. She honestly expressed that she was afraid of what this loss would mean for her and her family. This seemingly senseless loss had ripped a gaping hole in her heart, and she was struggling to find God in the midst of it all. As I listened to her share her grief, worries, and fear, I recognized so many of my own thoughts and feelings from just a few months earlier. When my family was in the middle of experiencing gut-wrenching loss, I struggled to make sense of it all. More often than not, my prayers in that season began with, "God, I don't understand." After listening to her share for some time, I started asking her a series of questions. I said, "Do you believe God knows and sees what you're going through?"

She said yes.

"Do you believe God cares about your family and loves you?"

She said yes.

"Do you believe God can bring something good and beautiful out of this season?"

She stayed silent for a moment.

I do not believe death was ever part of God's will. Sin and death entered the world because of man's choices, but death was never part of God's original plan. His original plan was for us to exist with Him in perfect communion in paradise—without sin, death, weeping, loss, sorrow, or sickness. Man's choices—not God's will—altered that beautiful and perfect picture. When someone said to me days after my sister had passed that it "must have just been God's will," I was angry. I do not believe it was God's will for my sister to have an allergic reaction to her medicine that would take her life and leave her 10-year-old daughter motherless. We live in a fallen world where things happen outside of God's will every moment of every day—even down to the smallest sin, people are regularly acting outside of God's will. People making decisions of their own free will, the constant decay of the world in which we live, and the effects of sin and death that entered the world when Eve took the fruit all crash together in one big mess outside of God's original plan. I believe God's original intent is what we will experience in heaven.

Revelation 21:4 gives us a glimpse of what we as Christ-followers have to look forward to:

"He will wipe every tear from their eyes, and there will

be no more death or sorrow or crying or pain. All these things are gone forever."

As Christians, the normality of the world—sin, death, grief, loss, pain, suffering—should feel oh so wrong to us. We were created to experience God's perfect will, which is no more death or loss or grief or suffering but rather, perfect and whole relationship with Him. This perfection and wholeness will be restored when we spend eternity with Him. Wow, I cannot wait until that day comes!

All of that to say, we live in a fallen world where sin and death still exist. There is still grief and pain, loss and suffering, *but* I also believe God is in the midst of it all—the sin, the grief, the brokenness—working His divine good. I believe God can bring the sweetest beauty out of the darkest seasons. Remember Romans 8:28? He does work all things together for the good of those who love Him and are called according to His purpose. When we surrender our mess into His hands, He will mold and shape something precious. Isaiah 61 talks about how the Lord will restore the beauty of Israel out of her ashes:

> The Spirit of the Sovereign Lord is on me, because the Lord has anointed me to proclaim good news to the poor. He has sent me to bind up the brokenhearted, to proclaim freedom for the captives and release from darkness for the prisoners, to proclaim the year of the Lord's favor and the day of vengeance of our God, to comfort all who mourn, and provide for those who grieve in Zion—to bestow on them a crown of beauty instead of ashes, the oil of joy instead of mourning, and a garment of praise instead of a spirit of despair. They will be called oaks of righteousness, a planting of the Lord for the display of His splendor. (Isaiah 61:1–3, NIV)

This Scripture paints a picture of despair, grief, loss, and hopelessness—sound a bit like our world today? But the Lord says that He is in it, and He will restore and renew what was broken. In fact, He calls us out of our brokenness. He says we will be "oaks of righteousness ... for the display of His splendor." As we continue to simply invite Him in, He will use the seasons of brokenness, despair, grief, and loss to display His splendor and glory in a way that would not have otherwise been possible. In all of the world's lowest places, He is still God and can display His glory.

That night with my friend, I continued to encourage her, saying that the Lord is in the midst of all of our grief and loss, and He can work something amazingly good in this situation, even if it wasn't part of His original plan. Some of God's best work has come out of the darkest brokenness and despair. And the next words that came out of my mouth surprised me as I said them: "Jesus was not part of God's original plan."

I had to pause for a moment as I sat on what the Lord had so clearly just spoken to my heart. Jesus was always with God and was always His beloved Son, but sending Him to earth to experience a sacrificial death on the cross was not part of God's original plan. Out of the world's worst brokenness—all of creation living in separation from their Creator—came the most beautiful gift and picture of restoration: Jesus. Look at what God can do in the worst possible scenario? He can bring the most unimaginable good. It was so far outside of His will for sin and death to enter the world, but His hand was in it all, working His good. Because of His goodness, we can now experience the fullness of relationship with Him through His perfect Son, Jesus, who died for us and loves us unconditionally. He is our Comforter, Prince of Peace, Intercessor before the Father, Healer, Deliverer, and so much more.

In the seasons of life when I only see brokenness and despair, I have to force myself to remember the most simple yet profound truth: the world saw only brokenness and suffering, but God saw a chance to send Jesus. I am learning to consciously refocus my thoughts about my present circumstances away from the grief and toward all the Lord can do because of His goodness and His hand in the midst of it.

Thankful for a Deeper Understanding

I am realizing that there are some aspects of the Lord's character and some lessons we will only learn through suffering and difficulty in this life. It is in the darkness of our suffering and hardship that we can more clearly see the radiance of His face. And in seasons of suffering, this thought brings me such hope and the most profound sense of peace. The Lord is so much greater than my circumstances, and when I choose to press into Him and *thank* Him, He can mold and shape my heart in ways that would not have otherwise been possible. He can bring the most beautiful good out of the seasons of darkest despair. When this shift happens in my mind, I turn my attention away from the brokenness and toward the hand of the Lord, moving in ways I cannot even see right now. My attitude becomes one of gratefulness— gratefulness that I serve a God who is in the midst of all of my despair and is working things for His perfect good. Thanksgiving in the darkness is far from my natural inclination, but it opens the door to this kingdom-perspective and a deeper intimacy with the Father.

Now trust me, I know better than most that this command to give a sacrifice of thanksgiving is not an easy thing to do at all. When I feel pain, frustration, or anger, the last thing I want to do is thank the Lord for it. I am in a season where thankfulness has not been the highest on my priority list. But the Lord has been obviously and continuously whispering to my heart that He is calling me to thankfulness in this season. He does not have me in a season where my circumstances are to change; He has me in a season for my circumstances to change me. Even the darkest of seasons can break open to reveal His hand and His glory. I can thank Him by faith that He is who He says He is. I can thank Him that history has proven to me that He will work it for my good. And I know He will do it again.

Opening the door to thankfulness—even when I don't feel like it—opens the door to His work in my heart. Thankfulness is what softens the clay, in essence, for the potter to begin to mold. His work will be beautiful—never forget, He promised it would bring Him glory. If He wants something to bring Him glory, you know He will make it beautiful. Simply choosing to say, "Lord, I am offering You my sacrifice of thanksgiving today," begins to open the door to the Lord in ways we could never imagine. It's an invitation that opens the channel from our hearts to the Lord's hands. It takes us back to the simple place of abiding in Him, trusting in His plan, and claiming His promises through every season. He desires to purify us so that His reflection is clearly seen, and a thankful heart is the road to get there. Simple, but oh, not easy.

What things—gifts or sacrifices—is the Lord calling me to be thankful for today?

_____

_____

_____

Heavenly Father, thank You for working tirelessly behind the scenes to accomplish Your good in my life. Help me maintain a thankful heart— for both the gifts You give and the trials I'm facing. Today, I choose to be thankful for (fill in the blank). Amen.

The key to understanding thankfulness amidst difficulty is recognizing that our thankfulness has more to do with *Who* we are thanking than *what* we are thankful for.

chapter 12

Simply Blessed...

I want to explore thankfulness on another level in this chapter. I believe thankfulness is one of the most vital pieces of the simplest thing in our relationship with the Lord, but it is so easily overlooked. Thankfulness is a direct invitation into relationship with the Lord. It is us making the active choice to say, "Lord, thank You for the work You are doing in my life." In times of joy and times of sorrow, this prayer opens our hearts to an intimacy with the Father.

Sometimes, thankfulness is a clear, cut-and-dry choice. I can choose to be thankful for the blessings I have received, or I can choose to offer up the sacrifice of thanksgiving for the trials I find myself in. But I believe there is still another side of thankfulness—thankfulness which arises from simply *recognizing* the blessings all around us.

Recognize the Blessings

On a superficial level, these simple blessings are the morning sun shining in the window, a really good cup of coffee, an unexpected text from an old friend, a walk in the fresh air, or a smile from a stranger. They're small. They could slip by unnoticed. But when they're recognized, they bring the purest form of joy into a moment.

On a much deeper level, we are already and eternally blessed by the Father. Ephesians 1:3 says,

> "All praise to God, the Father of our Lord Jesus Christ, who has blessed us with every spiritual blessing in the heavenly realms because we are united with Christ."

Notice the past-tense in this verse: "has blessed us ...." It's already been done and completed. God has blessed us with every spiritual blessing because we are united with Christ. How many times a day does that slip past me unnoticed? More than I'd care to admit. Friends, we are simply blessed by our Father with every spiritual blessing. We need only to claim it and thank Him for it.

And please listen, friends, *it really is just that easy.* The only responsibility on us is to rest and abide in His promises, thanking Him for these blessings. Once we have done our part to let go of striving and rest in His care and sovereignty, it is the job of the Holy Spirit to minister to us, strengthen us, equip us, comfort us, guide us, correct us, and teach us the more profound things of God. We need only to claim every spiritual blessing and thank Him for it.

Yet, I understand so well that many times, circumstances scream the opposite to us. We might already be blessed, but we don't always *feel* blessed in a moment. And the Lord understands this—He created us, He created our minds, and He created our feelings. But each time we rest in His care and take a step of thankfulness for His promises despite our feelings, we are taking a bold step of faith and claiming His promises.

Blessings That Slip By

With the frenetic pace at which I often find my life running, it's painfully easy for thankfulness to slip my mind. I experience the blessing and take it in stride while often forgetting to cherish it and express thankfulness. I think this is where the phrase "practicing thankfulness" found its roots. I'm sad to say that it's not often a natural response to be thankful but rather something we must practice. And I'm not just talking about the big blessings—though we certainly need to be grateful for those!—I'm talking about the blessings that slip by unnoticed yet have the profound ability to impact a moment.

The other morning, I got up early to do some reading before I left for the office. As I opened my curtains, I saw that it had snowed a bit the night before. I was living in Texas, so the snow was a true phenomenon. It might have only been a light dusting, but for this Colorado girl, it was enough to warm my heart and bring a little unexpected joy to my day.

As I sat in my chair drinking my coffee and looking out at the little bit of snow remaining, I felt the Lord whisper to my heart, "Just take a moment to enjoy it. It's a blessing." Thankfulness welled up in my heart. So many times in my life, I watch for blessings and hope they'll peek out from time to time, yet I miss some of the sweetest gifts simply because they're unexpected or not what I was looking for.

Blessings That Look Different from What We Pictured

In Exodus 16, Moses had just led the Israelites out of Egypt to their freedom, and they were entering the wilderness. Just over a month after their liberation, the people ran out of food and began to complain that they would die of starvation, wishing they were back in Egypt. The Lord heard their cries and promised to provide food.

Side note: the Israelites weren't asking nicely. They

were angry, they were complaining, and they were, in essence, saying that they wished the Lord hadn't miraculously saved them from slavery. Even so, the Lord heard them, took compassion on them, and provided for their needs. This doesn't mean that we should approach the Lord with grumbling and complaining, but even on our worst days when that's all that seems to come out of our mouths, the Lord still hears, still loves, and still provides. What a good, good Father we serve.

The next morning, the people woke and saw manna covering the ground, but it was like nothing they had ever seen before. They asked, "What is it?" Moses had to explain that this was the bread the Lord had given them to eat. What a blessing. This wasn't even a small one that could be easily missed—this was the Lord miraculously saving them from starvation! But because it wasn't what they expected, they almost missed it. Truthfully, I cannot fault them. How many times in my own life have I asked the Lord for provision but almost missed it because it came in a package that was different than what I was expecting?

In my life, I've often found myself saying, "I feel like most of my blessings are just blessings in disguise." You know what I mean? Things that seem really difficult, painful, or hurtful at the moment, but once you're on the other side looking back, you see all you've learned, all the Lord has taught you, and all the ways you've grown because of them. They're blessings in disguise.

I've often felt frustrated—like my lot in life was all blessings in disguise and no blessings just for the sake of blessings. How wrong I was. The blessings I was hoping for and watching for were distracting me from seeing the gifts I was given every day. I was looking for answers and blessings that matched what I had constructed in my head and could not see the gifts the Lord was giving me along the way. How sad and unfulfilling. I missed out on the ability to fully receive and enjoy so many blessings and the opportunity to thank my Father for them because I was expecting something different.

Change What We See

I was reading in the Psalms the other day, and Psalm 30:11 stood out to me:

> "You have turned my mourning into joyful dancing. You have taken away my clothes of mourning and clothed me with joy."

This verse simply sings of answered prayers, faithfulness, and blessings. I began to pray, "Lord, let that be my prayer! Would You move in my life and turn my mourning into joyful dancing—would You clothe me with joy!" As I sought the Lord, I felt the prayer of my heart begin to shift from "turn my mourning into joyful dancing" to "open my eyes to see the places of my life that I can shed my clothes of mourning and put on clothes of joy." When I'm not intentionally shifting my focus to the unexpected blessings, I seem to remain laser-focused on my "clothes of mourning."

How much grief, disappointment, loneliness, depression, and heaviness do we carry around with us unnecessarily because our eyes have not been opened to the unexpected blessings?

Let's pause here for a moment. Try as we might, there are just things we cannot see or understand on our own. But, my friends, this isn't a moment to feel guilty because we just can't seem to see the goodness of God! No! This is a moment to *invite Him in*. Ephesians 1:18 says,

> "I pray that your hearts will be flooded with light so that you can understand the confident hope he has given to those he called—his holy people who are his rich and glorious inheritance."

My friends, He will flood our hearts with light so we can understand the hope we have in Him. We are His people, blessed with His inheritance. He longs for us to understand that. As we take a step back from striving and invite Him in, He will begin to open our eyes to recognize the blessings—the spiritual, the simple, and the big.

In 2 Kings 6, the king of Aram sent horses, chariots, and "a strong force" to surround the city where Elisha and his servant were staying. The servant became terrified, but Elisha responded in verse 16, "'Those who are with us are more than those who are with them'" (NIV). Then Elisha prayed that the Lord would open his servant's eyes. When the servant looked around, he saw that the hills were full of horses and chariots of fire all around Elisha. On his own, the servant couldn't see the supernatural protection with his natural eye; he needed the Lord to open his eyes. Sometimes—many times—we need the Lord to open our eyes to see what He is doing around us.

In reality, this is where you and I live every single day. Scripture tells us we have been blessed, forgiven, chosen, adopted, redeemed, accepted—past tense! But until our spiritual eyes are opened to see these supernatural truths, we will not see ourselves as blessed, forgiven, chosen, adopted, redeemed, accepted ... the list goes on. Invite Him in to open your eyes.

Watch for the Unexpected Answers

When our eyes are not opened to see the ways the Lord is working around us, we carry around burdens that are not ours to bear. But let's take it a step further—how much do we carry around with us because the Lord has actually *answered* our prayer in a way we didn't expect, and our eyes aren't open to see that?

I don't think the blind man Jesus healed expected Jesus to spit in the dirt, make mud, and wipe it on his eyes. What if instead, he had waited around for Jesus to say, "Eyes, be opened!" and then never opened his eyes because he thought he wasn't healed? This no-longer-blind man would have been walking around with perfect sight, but his eyes were closed because Jesus didn't heal him in the way he expected to be healed. He would have been walking around in his clothes of mourning, thinking he was still blind instead of dancing for joy because his sight was restored!

A New Prayer

I will always pray for the Lord to move in my life. I will always pray when I experience grief, face significant life decisions, struggle in a relationship, or need divine provision. But the Lord is teaching me to accompany those prayers with another one: "Lord, open my eyes to see where You are at work in my life. Through the help of the Holy Spirit, help me to see the blessings You are giving me and the answers You are bringing—especially when they look different than I expect." When we thank Him by faith for who He is, even when our eyes tell us a different story, we give Him the most incredible honor we can. Psalm 30:11 asks the Lord to exchange the mourning for joy, and Psalm 30:12 reminds us why: "that I might sing praises to you and not be silent. O Lord my God, I will give you thanks forever!"

In our pursuit of practicing a thankful heart, I think we must start asking the Lord to open our eyes to see the unexpected blessings—both big and small. When we're not watching for them or when they look different from what we were expecting, we miss them as we rush through our days. We miss the opportunity to fully receive a blessing, and we miss the opportunity to thank our gracious Father, who gave it to us simply because He loved us. As my mom always says, "Watch for God!"

This takes us directly back to the simple act of inviting the Lord into each moment of each day. As I make the conscious decision to invite Him into a moment, I am taking my focus off what I can see around me and shifting it to the Father, His work, and who He is to me. When we rest on who He says He is to us and the promises of Scripture, we can recognize that we are simply blessed at any moment and in any situation. In the Psalms alone, He says He is ...

Our Shield,
Our Refuge,
Our faithful Friend,
The Lover of our soul,
A High Tower we can enter into for safety.

When the storms of life come, we must declare His promises and thank Him for who He says He is to us. No matter how things look or feel, that is faith that pleases God. Philippians 4:6 reminds us that we don't have to be anxious about anything. We can remember that we are simply blessed as we bring Him our concerns and cares.

When I choose to rest in Him, I am saying, "Not my will, but Yours be done."

When I abide in Him, I am asking for His eyes to see the world around me.

When we consciously invite the Lord into a moment, I believe our perspectives shift much more clearly from what *we see* as our current circumstances to the *Lord's view*.

In our own efforts and from our earthly perspectives,

there are times when we are truly blind to the work the Lord is doing in and around us. As we intentionally invite Him into the moment, we begin to see things as He sees them, even though they may look different from what we pictured initially. As the Lord begins to open our eyes more and more to the blessings around us—small and unexpected—we are enabled to thank Him more. The simple practice of inviting Him in, abiding in Him, and resting in His presence begins to open our eyes to see the unexpected blessings. As we recognize those blessings and return to Him with a thankful heart, we open ourselves up even more for our Father to work in us. A thankful heart is a conduit of His work. The more we recognize this and engage in thankfulness, the more our hearts and minds are transformed. The practice of thanksgiving slowly begins to shift into an attitude of thanksgiving.

What blessings—the simple and the spiritual—have been slipping by me unnoticed?

_____

_____

_____

_____

Heavenly Father, thank You for showering me with blessings each day. Would You open my eyes to see where You are at work in my life? Through the Holy Spirit, help me to see the blessings You are giving me and the answers You are bringing—especially when they look different than I expect. Amen

As we take a step back from striving and invite Him in, He will begin to open our eyes to recognize the blessings—the spiritual, the simple, and the big.

chapter 13

Simply Hoping...

As I sit down to write this chapter, I am in the middle of one of the strangest and most unexpected seasons of my life. We are facing a global pandemic: COVID-19. The speed and intensity with which this virus took hold of the world are truly shocking. There are so many reports out about its effects, its severity, and its lasting impact. Regardless of which side of the fence you fall on, this pandemic disrupted lives across the globe. For the first time in my lifetime, and really, history all across the world, we are experiencing the same thing at the same time. What a strange time we're living in.

This pandemic and its effects have unearthed fear, doubt, hopelessness, discouragement, and anger in the hearts of so many. And let me tell you, simplicity has been tossed out the window. Can I get an amen?

Do I wear a mask? Do I not wear a mask?
Do I go to the store? If I go to the store, I need to make sure I'm
walking in the correct direction down the right aisles.
Do I gather with my friends and family?
Do I attend church in person or watch online?
Do I go back to work or request to work remotely?
Do I send my children back to school?

> *Our governor is telling us one thing, but our mayor tells us*
> *something different—what should I do?*
> *Is this a conspiracy?*
> *In the midst of all of this, racial tensions are at an all-time high.*
> *Should I lend my voice to the conversations? If so, how?*
> *Wait, what about murder hornets??*
> *Did someone say a giant sandstorm is blowing to the U.S. all*
> *the way from the Sahara?*
> *Is this the End Times?*
> *One report says this, but another report from an equally reputable*
> *source tells me the exact opposite!*
> *I don't know who or what to believe.*

It's stressing me out enough just rereading what I've written, much less living through it! Everywhere we turn, people are talking about the virus. The news is filled with reports, churches are navigating their responses, government officials are putting out press releases at the speed of lightning, and simple conversations with those closest to us are centered around "the times we're living in." Sometimes I sit down and try to remember what we talked about before coronavirus.

Simplicity, it seems, is a thing of the past. Remember that feeling I talked about at the very beginning of our journey together? The feeling of knowing I have so much to bring before the Lord—to pray about—but not knowing where to begin? That feeling is creeping back into my mornings with the Lord. And one of the things keeping me most grounded is *The Simplest Thing...* Each time I'm tempted to feel overwhelmed and unsure of what to do, I'm reminded of this beautiful lesson the Lord is still teaching me: *just invite Him in.*

I've found any time the Lord is asking me to teach on something, I'm tested in that very thing. I'm deep in this book; I'm praying over the content; I'm seeking the Lord for

His words and heart to share with you, so of course, this very message is going to be tested in my heart.

> *Do I really believe that the most pivotal point in my relationship with the Lord is something so simple?*
> *Do I really believe that the key to intimacy with the Creator of the Universe is inviting Him in and abiding in Him?*
> *Is He really my source of strength when all hell seems to break loose?*

Honestly? Sometimes I need to be reminded.

Where Am I Allowing My Mind to Dwell?

A few weeks into our shelter-in-place order, I was feeling particularly overwhelmed and discouraged. I was dwelling on the circumstances surrounding me. Remember, to *dwell* somewhere means that we remain for a time in that place, live there as a resident, or keep our attention directed on it. I had definitely taken up residence, focusing on everything going on around me, particularly the things that I felt were not going the way I thought they should. I was just disappointed and discouraged. I couldn't shake it. You know those days?

This feeling persisted for a few days, and I was getting sick of it. I sat down with my cable-knit blanket and my coffee, and I asked the Lord, "Why am I feeling so discouraged?" I follow the Bible in One Year plan on the Bible App, and I turned to my reading for that day—Psalm 43. When I hit verse 5, I couldn't help but chuckle:

> "Why am I discouraged? Why is my heart so sad? I will put my hope in God! I will praise him again—my Savior and my God!"

Oh! Well, thanks, Lord. Don't you love it when you ask a question and open your Bible to the exact answer? It doesn't happen to me often, but I cherish it when it does.

As I studied the chapter in full, I found so many parallels for my current season or almost any season we find ourselves in:

> Declare me innocent, O God! Defend me against these ungodly people. Rescue me from these unjust liars. For you are God, my only safe haven. Why have you tossed me aside? Why must I wander around in grief, oppressed by my enemies? Send out your light and your truth; let them guide me. Let them lead me to your holy mountain, to the place where you live. There I will go to the altar of God, to God—the Source of all my joy. I will praise you with my harp, O God, my God! Why am I discouraged? Why is my heart so sad? I will put my hope in God! I will praise him again—my Savior and my God! (Psalm 43)

From one minute to the next, we can be singing praises to Him for His faithfulness and then questioning if He remembers we exist. Can I propose a thought? We are a people of fickle feelings. Like the psalmist in chapter 43, we look around us, and it's easy to feel overwhelmed:

> "Defend me against these ungodly people. Rescue me from these unjust liars. ... I wander around in grief, oppressed by my enemies."

When we look around us at the world today—especially in this unique season of a global pandemic—it is so easy to want to focus on our need for rescue. It's easy to feel grief. And discouragement? Well, it seems to waltz right on in uninvited. Whether you've been a Christ-follower for 10 minutes or 10 years, discouragement is that thing to which none of us are really ever immune.

In that moment alone with my coffee, the Lord began revealing to me the object of my focus. He gently showed me that I was hoping *for* a lot of things more than I was putting my hope *in* Him. As I focused on what was going on around me and on the fact that things were not coming to pass the way I thought they should, I began to slowly abandon my simple invitation to the Lord to come in and work amidst my circumstances. I was flinging the door wide open for discouragement to waltz on in, and this time, it was invited.

Proverbs 13:12 says that hope deferred makes the heart sick. Every time we feel that sickness of heart—discouragement—yellow flashing lights and sirens should be going off in our spirits. It works as our warning signal, highlighting when we misplace our focus on our hopes instead of our God.

The Gift of Hope in the Right Place

It's a beautiful thing to hope, and there are so many things we are hoping for! Marriage, family, jobs, ministry opportunities, a home, financial stability ... and it's not wrong to hope for any of these things! But the key is, are we hoping for these things *more* than we are hoping in the Lord? If we hope for things more than the Lord, we can be prone to settle or head in a direction the Lord never intended for us to go.

And this isn't merely a problem that you and I face today. The father of our faith met it, himself! God promised Abraham that he would have a son, but Abraham placed so much hope in the promise that he took his focus off the Provider. Abraham thought he needed to take things into his own hands to bring about the promise, and that involved a way the Lord never intended for him to take. Abraham's decision to have a son by his wife's servant caused division in his family and, ultimately, between two nations. His hope became misplaced, and the result was a torn version of the promise.

When we get caught up hoping for specific things, we head in our own direction, pull and resist when God might be moving us somewhere else, or get discouraged when we feel like circumstances around us aren't matching up to the way we think things should be. When we hope in God above all else, offering that sacrifice of thanksgiving and thanking Him by faith for who He is to us, we keep our eyes on Him, trusting Him to fulfill our hopes in His perfect way and His perfect time. In the waiting, when I'm tempted to give in to fear, frustration, or impatience, I'm reminded to invite Him in and thank Him for who He says He is to me.

As I pondered this revelation, it reminded me of a time several years ago when I took my horse out of her pasture to graze on some fresh, green grass. While she had a large field to roam as she pleased, she had pretty well eaten up all of the grass over those few acres. She had most certainly been faithful with what she was given ....

I found her in the pasture, put on her halter, and led her through the gate. I had a particular section of our property in mind that was literally overrun with thick, tall, green grass. However, as we walked along, she continually stopped and grabbed at the tiny shoots of grass along the way. They were sparse, to be sure, but better than what she'd had in the pasture. I had to keep tugging on the lead and physically pulling her head up to keep her moving.

Finally, I said to her, "Girl, if only you knew where I'm taking you. Please, *just trust me*. It's so much better than this." As soon as the words left my mouth, I heard the Lord whisper to my heart, "Did you hear what you just said?" I said, "Yes, Sir."

How many times in our walk with the Lord do we get so

caught up in the circumstances around us that we lose sight of where He may be trying to lead us? Things may seem so easy and comfortable—inviting—that we resist His gentle leading toward something even better.

Or how many times do we feel so overwhelmed by our circumstances that we just want to lie down and give up because we see no way out? We forsake the simplicity of following Him for the complexity of trying to figure out the current circumstances and future outcomes on our own! But in both of these cases and more, the Lord is calling us simply to abide in Him, invite Him in, and trust His leading. When we choose the antithesis, we dwell in stagnation, disappointment, and fear.

Hope for the Giver Above the Gift

That day with my Bible open in the middle of the pandemic, I felt so convicted that my hope was laser-focused on specific *things* instead of on the Lord, Himself. I was seeking His gifts, but those gifts weren't coming around how I thought they should. And as we all know, things don't always work out the way we think is best. The Lord longs to give us good gifts as we walk through life with Him. Matthew 7:11 says,

> "So if you sinful people know how to give good gifts to your children, how much more will your heavenly Father give good gifts to those who as him."

He longs to bless us richly and abundantly! He is a good, good Father. But sometimes, His gifts look different than we expect. Or He withholds what we think would be oh so good at the moment for something that's coming that He knows is even better. He is gently leading us along, whispering to us: "If you only knew where I'm taking you. Please, just trust Me. It's so much better than this."

Psalm 43:3 says, "Send out your light and your truth; let them guide me. Let them lead me to your holy mountain, to the place where you live."

When we keep our attention on His light and dwell on His truth, He leads us directly to the place where He lives. He brings us in close communion with Him. He *abides* with us. Verse 4 says in that place is our Source of joy. When we abide in Him, rest in Him, invite Him in, and trust Him to lead us, we are actively choosing to hope in Him. When we make this choice, joy is birthed in our hearts regardless of what the circumstances around us say.

When we take our focus off Him, off what we know is true about Him and His Father-heart, and when we focus on the seeming discrepancy between what we're hoping for and our current circumstances, discouragement takes up residence, puts down roots, sets up camp. We have invited it in when we hope for the gift over the Giver. Pure hope is longing for the Giver above the gift.

My friends, we're on a journey with the Lord. Our entire life is a walk with Him. We can choose to walk in the opposite direction, we can choose to walk keeping Him at arms-length, or we can choose to invite the Father in to walk hand-in-hand with us, remaining attentive to His every step and direction.

We will inevitably see the circumstances surrounding us on this life-long walk if we keep our eyes open. And truthfully, I believe we should be aware of what's going on around us. Matthew 24:42 urges us to stay awake and alert as we watch for the coming of the Lord. We shouldn't be ostriches that shove their heads down in the sand at the first sign of trouble. But when we choose to keep our heads out of the sand and alert to the circumstances surrounding us, the temptation toward discouragement creeps in. How do we balance perceiving the circumstances with not allowing them to overwhelm us? The key is that our hand never leaves His. As we take each step, despite the circumstances, we are stepping in tune with the Father. The Father who sees the future, sees how every event—the beautiful and the ugly—can be used for His glory, and sees the part He has designed for us to play.

As we ask Him daily to send us His light and His truth, He will bring us into His place of dwelling. As the attitude of our heart shifts steadily toward walking in step with Him, we abide with Him. As we invite Him into every circumstance, whether we can pinpoint exactly where He is at work or not, we slam the door in the face of discouragement, for discouragement cannot take root in a heart that is so fully enraptured with the truth and promises of the Father. We believe that even when we cannot see it, He is working. Even when we cannot feel it, He is working ("Waymaker"). As we choose to see and recognize what's going on around us yet still choose to simply abide in the Father and rest in Him, we experience true hope.

In what areas of my life am I feeling discouraged right now?

_____

_____

_____

_____

Heavenly Father, thank You for being faithful and my true Source of hope. Forgive me for hoping for (list the things above) more than placing my hope in You. Would You help me to reorder my thoughts to focus on You and remind me of Your promises to which I can cling as I wait? Amen.

*Pure hope
is longing
for the Giver
above the gift.*

chapter 14

Simply Taken Care of...

———

Over the past few months, one of my prayers has been that the Lord would give me a deeper understanding of who He is. I firmly believe there are aspects of the Lord's nature that we will not grasp with logic and human knowledge. In 1 Corinthians 2, it talks about the Holy Spirit knowing the deep things of God and revealing them to us. I like the way the New Living Translation phrases verse 10:

> "But it was to us that God revealed these things by his Spirit. For his Spirit searches out everything and shows us God's deep secrets."

There are many aspects of God that we will not be able to understand in our own minds; they will require the revelation of the Holy Spirit. Even understanding the love of God fully—Paul prays in Ephesians 3:19 that we would have the power to comprehend the depth of God's love toward us, even though it is too vast to understand completely.

Partner with God in the Process

There is a lot about God that we *must* have the revelation of the Holy Spirit to understand. *Caveat: we cannot just ask for a deeper understanding and then go on our merry ways with no intention of cultivating that deeper understanding.* The first and most important step in deepening our relationship with the Lord will always be to invite Him in, abide in Him, and rest in relationship with Him. I also believe that there are things we can—must—do to further our understanding. Saint Augustine even said, "Pray as though everything depended on God. Work as though everything depended on you." So, in pursuit of my prayer to understand more of Jesus, I decided to read the Gospels—what better way to learn more about the Lord than to read the four books explicitly written about Him?

In my reading, I loved learning how Jesus would respond in situations. His love, grace, and justice were evident through each circumstance He found Himself in and each parable He taught.

His messages revealed revolutionary thoughts about God—presenting Him as a loving Father.

He taught about the coming kingdom.

He healed the sick and freed the oppressed.

He lavished love on all those around Him.

As I read the Gospels, however, something else caught my attention: the responses of the disciples. It intrigued me to read of their amazing responses of faith, the way several of them left everything and everyone they knew to follow Jesus, and the times when they cried out in fear or questioned Jesus. I think you could find just about any human emotion or response at one time or another in the disciples: faith, love, trust, hope, fear, disappointment, anger, doubt ... their responses make them feel a little more relatable. But there were times in my reading that their responses seemed a little unreasonable, even to a girl who feels the full spectrum of human emotions in her relationship with the Lord on a regular basis.

The Wrongness of Our Circumstances Sets the Stage for His Work

One such story recently caught my attention: when Jesus feeds the four thousand. In Matthew 15, Jesus is teaching a large crowd on the mountainside. He teaches and heals over a period of three days, and Jesus feels compassion on them for they have had nothing to eat. The disciples respond: "Where would we get enough food here in the wilderness for such a huge crowd?" (Matthew 15:33). That seems like a pretty natural question, right? I think I would be asking the same thing.

This is one of those times when it feels like things are going downhill pretty quickly. The time of ministry started out great! Jesus was on the move—teaching and healing. But now, they were all tired and hungry, and they were far from any source of food or shelter. You know those days that start out great, but quickly it begins to feel like nothing is going right? Even as I write this, it's been a day. All started out well! But now, I'm sitting down to start writing three hours later than I hoped to start; the coffee shop made me the wrong drink; it was too hot to sit outside so I moved inside, but it's too loud inside; and for some reason, the audio on my computer isn't loud enough for my worship music to drown out the noise. And these were just the frustrating little cherries on top of what had become an already disheveled day. I just can't seem to focus, and I feel a little overwhelmed. I also feel defeated … I wanted to write today, but I feel flustered and don't know that I have much to give.

Now, comparatively, I would say the day the disciples were having was a little heavier than mine, but still, a day where things seemed to be going downhill pretty quickly. I can imagine them asking themselves questions like, "Why did Jesus have to start preaching so far from town?" or "Why couldn't He have wrapped up sooner so that people could go home?" or "Why didn't these people think to bring food?" I would guess they felt discouraged, overwhelmed, and a little defeated, and I can't blame them. I would be asking questions, too.

Generally, their responses make sense. However, what baffles me a bit is that exactly one chapter before, Jesus fed five thousand hungry people. Remember in chapter 14, Matthew records Jesus instructing the disciples to find food for the multitude. They turn up with five loaves of bread and two fish, and Jesus performs a miracle so that all five thousand men (and more including the women and children) ate and were satisfied. There were even twelve basketfuls of leftovers.

We don't know exactly how much time took place between Jesus feeding the five thousand and then feeding the four thousand, but we do know that Jesus' ministry on earth was three years long. Whether there was a day in between these two miracles, a month, or three full years, I would think the disciples would remember Jesus' provision. A lot has happened in the last three years of my life. Still, I can pretty much guarantee you I would remember a time when I had to unexpectedly feed five thousand people with five loaves of bread and two fish, and the Lord miraculously multiplied it all before my eyes to the point that I had *twelve* baskets of leftovers. (I always thought it was interesting that there were twelve baskets of leftovers and twelve disciples, but that may be another conversation for another time.)

In short, as I read the account of Jesus feeding the four thousand—even with the frustrating circumstances—it's hard not to think that the disciples were *ridiculous* to ask, "Where could we get enough bread in this remote place to feed such a crowd?" How could you forget that Jesus literally just came through for you and fed a crowd much bigger than this? As I pondered this, my finger pointed firmly toward the disciples began to slowly shift back toward me. How many times have I fearfully run to the Lord with a problem, begging Him for an answer, when He has already made provision for that problem and so many more? How many times do I forget His faithfulness to provide in the impossible? How often do I doubt His goodness to provide again?

As I sat in the coffee shop feeling discouraged, I started to complain to the Lord: "It feels like so much is going wrong today. Why can't things just go right for once?"

Almost instantly, I heard Him say, "But things are going right with Me."

When the disciples had to feed the four thousand, everything was going right with the Lord. He had a plan, and He used the wrongness of the circumstances to bring Himself even more glory.

When His only Son was going to the cross, the circumstances felt so far beyond wrong. Jesus was the promised Messiah who was supposed to save Israel from her enemies, and He was dying the brutal death of a criminal. But still, everything was going right with God.

When my family experienced gut-wrenching pain and loss twice in a matter of days, it felt like everything was going wrong. But still, somehow, I hear God whisper, "But everything is right with Me." This doesn't mean that death was God's will; in fact, I believe quite the opposite—death was never part of His original plan. But it does mean that even though the circumstances seem all wrong—horrifically wrong—things can still be right with God.

Our Responses Shift the Attitude of Our Hearts

Even when their responses seem ridiculous, upon further

reflection, I realize that the disciples are still relatable. If I look more closely at my own life, I see that some of my own responses are indeed ridiculous.

I run to the Lord with a problem full of fear of the unknown, when instead, I should run to the Lord with my problem full of faith that He will provide the answer.

I feel overwhelmed by the weight of my problem when I should be inviting Him in and casting my cares on Him, for He cares for me (1 Peter 5:7).

I worry about how the problem will be resolved when I should be resting peacefully, knowing that He has been faithful before, so He will be faithful again (even if this time around, it looks different).

I complain about how my circumstances seem all wrong, when I should walk forward with confidence, knowing that things are still right with my God because Jesus is the same yesterday, today, and forever.

So often, I respond as the disciples did, even though I can look back and point out distinct markers of the Lord's faithfulness and provision in my own life. I seem to quickly forget the promises He has given me, the times He has been faithful before, and the truth He has revealed to my heart through His Word. I suppose I have little to judge them for. But I love that even with all of their doubting and fear, the Lord still does a miracle. He still listens, He still moves, He still *provides*.

Simply Returning to the Father

As I sit in this coffee shop, I feel Him asking me if I trust Him based on my feelings which are dictated by unstable circumstances, or if my trust in Him is based on the stability of His faithfulness and His promises. He says in His Word that He has a good plan for us, He directs our steps, He hears our cries, and He will never leave or forsake us.

I may not always *feel* that truth with the changing of my circumstances, but I can build my trust in Him on the truth of His promises and monuments of His faithfulness in the past. His faithfulness has nothing to do with us or what we do. He won't be faithful merely because we've rallied our emotions to believe He is. And He won't withhold His promises just because we may forget. Can you imagine the fickleness of our circumstances if the Lord's faithfulness were dependent upon us? And so much work! I would be eternally exhausted if the Lord's commitment to me depended on what I did or did not do. Praise God that the message of the gospel is the antithesis of this. We aren't responsible for the Lord's faithfulness; we are responsible for settling down in our spirits and resting in the Father. As I abide in Him, there is a strength that comes from deep in my spirit.

> I know He has been faithful.
> I know He is faithful.
> I know He will be faithful again.
> I know because I rest in Him.

Instead of feeling disappointed in myself for forgetting the Lord's goodness in my life, I want to take this opportunity to remind myself of His faithfulness. The Lord knows better than we do the ways our minds struggle with fear and uncertainty—He created them. Instead of wallowing in shame and guilt for so quickly forgetting, He wants us to take it as an opportunity to *return* to Him.

> To return to the simplicity of inviting Him in.
> The simplicity of resting under the shadow of His wing.
> The simplicity of trusting that we can lean on Him as
> our firm foundation.

He wants to use these moments to remind us that, no matter what trials we face—whether they seem more significant than the last—we can rest in the promise that all is right with Him, and we are simply taken care of.

I believe the Lord has me on a never-ending journey of learning the simplest thing ... I don't know that I will ever stop needing to return to square one of inviting Him into each moment.

I am still learning to invest in my relationship with Him, to be brave in my waiting, and to hand Him my mess so He can mold and shape beauty.

I am still learning that relationship with my God will not always be easy. There will be sacrifices of thanksgiving, seasons of cultivation, and times when the earth shakes and mountains crumble.

My relationship with the Lord is often far from black and white, it frequently lacks a clear-cut plan with well-defined action steps, and I rarely know what is coming next, but let me tell you, this roller-coaster of faith has been the most rewarding and beautiful ride of my life. The ups and downs are causing me to cling to Him in ways I never knew I needed to, and each time, He proves Himself faithful. He shows me that I am simply taken care of, and I can stand on His promises and place my hope in Him whether or not my fickle feelings match up.

But more than anything, I am still learning that my relationship with the Lord is not dependent upon eloquent prayers, lavish displays of affection, or grandiose acts of service. As I continue to pray for a deeper revelation of the Lord and who He is to me, He is showing me that my relationship with Him, while not always easy, is simple. It hinges on the first step of inviting Him in, abiding in Him, and resting my soul in Him, and that, my friends, is the simplest thing ....

As we come to the end of our journey of *The Simplest Thing…*, think back over the last few weeks, months, or even years. What are the monuments of God's faithfulness in your life?

_____

_____

_____

_____

Pause and reflect on what you wrote down and carry your words with you as reminders that our God is faithful.

Heavenly Father, thank You for always being faithful. Forgive me for doubting Your faithfulness because of my fickle feelings. Help me to remember the monuments I've written down. Today, I choose to invite You in, abide in You, and rest my soul in You. Amen.

We aren't responsible
for the Lord's
faithfulness; we are
responsible for
settling down in our
spirits and resting
in the Father.

Other Works Mentioned

Bevere, John. *God, Where Are You?!* Palmer Lake, CO: Messenger International, Inc., 2019.

Lewis, C. S. *Till We Have Faces.* London: William Collins, 2020.

Lewis, C. S., and Clyde S. Kilby. *Letters to an American Lady.* Grand Rapids, MI: William B. Eerdmans Publishing Company, 2014.

Lewis, C. S. *Mere Christianity.* London: William Collins, 2017.

Mulholland, M. Robert, and R. Ruth Barton. *Invitation to a Journey.* Downers Grove, IL: InterVarsity Press, 2016.

Murray, Andrew. *Absolute Surrender.* La Vergne: Antiquarius, 2021.

Piper, John. *Desiring God.* Sisters, OR: Multinomah Books, 1996.

Tozer, A. W. *Knowledge of the Holy.* Bibliotech Press, 2019.

Made in the USA
Las Vegas, NV
22 January 2022

42016519R00121